Native North Americans

Native North Americans

A Supplement to
Childcraft—The How and Why Library

World Book, Inc.
a Scott Fetzer company
Chicago

For information about other World Book publications, visit our Web site **http://www.worldbook.com**, or call **1-800-WORLDBK (967-5325)**. For information about sales to schools and libraries, call **1-800-975-3250 (United States); 1-800-837-5365 (Canada)**.

World Book, Inc.
233 N. Michigan Ave.
Chicago, IL 60601
U.S.A.

Library of Congress Cataloging-in-Publication Data

Native North Americans: a supplement to Childcraft--the how and why library.
    p. cm.
  Includes bibliographical references and index.
  ISBN 0-7166-0608-9
   1. Indians of North America--History. 2. Indians of North America--Folklore.
3. Indians of North America--Social life and customs. I. World Book, Inc.
II. Childcraft.

E77.4.N37 2004
970.004'9--dc22

                                              2004002278

Printed in the United States of America
1 2 3 4 5 6 7 8 9 09 08 07 06 05 04

Staff

President and Publisher
Robert C. Martin

Vice President, Editorial
Dominic J. Miccolis

Editor-in-Chief
Dale W. Jacobs

**Managing Editor,
World Book Publishing**
Paul A. Kobasa

Editorial
**Managing Editor,
General Publishing & Annuals**
Maureen Mostyn Liebenson

Associate Editor
Shawn Brennan

Writers
Kathleen E. Kain
Mary Kayaian
Sara F. Shacter

Indexing Services
David Pofelski

Permissions Editor
Janet T. Peterson

Research
Manager, Research Services
Loranne K. Shields

Chief Researcher, Special Projects
Cheryl Graham

Art
Manager, Graphics and Design
Sandra M. Dyrlund

Designer
Anne Fritzinger

Contributing Designer
Lucy Lesiak

Contributing Photographs Editor
Carol Parden

**Production and
Administrative Support**
John Whitney

Production
**Director,
Manufacturing and Pre-Press**
Carma Fazio

Manufacturing Manager
Barbara Podczerwinski

Senior Production Manager
Madelyn Underwood

Production/Technology Manager
Jared Svoboda

Proofreader
Anne Dillon

Text Processing
Curley Hunter
Gwendolyn Johnson

World Book thanks the following individuals for their contributions to *Native North Americans:*

Professor Donald L. Fixico
*Thomas Bowlus Distinguished
  Professor of American Indian History
Editor of* Indigenous Nations
  Studies Journal
*Department of History
University of Kansas
Lawrence, KS*

Professor Alan L. Kolata
*Department of Anthropology
University of Chicago
Chicago, IL*

Contents

Introduction to
Native North Americans

This book is about Native Americans in North America. It describes 10 groups and shows how greatly the groups differed from one another. Life for a Tlingit boy on the western coast of Canada was not at all like that of a Hopi girl in the southwestern part of the United States, or an Aztec boy in Mexico. How each group lived depended very much upon where it lived.

The stories about these groups will show you where these people came from. You will see how they lived before Europeans came to their land, and you will learn about their descendants today.

In addition to facts, *Native North Americans* contains legends. Storytelling was—and continues to be—important to Native Americans as a way of sharing their history and knowledge with their children and grandchildren.

Native North Americans features hands-on activities and games, too. Biographies of interesting and important contemporary Native Americans are also scattered throughout the book. The back of the book includes a Glossary to help you understand unfamiliar terms and an Index to help you find information quickly. Finally, you can learn about other books, Web sites, and computer games that focus on Native Americans in the "Find Out More" section. Your parents and teachers might also find this list of additional resources helpful.

Tlingit

Inuit

Blackfeet

Ojibwa

Pomo

Iroquois

Osage

Hopi

Cherokee

Aztec

The map shows where each group discussed in the book lived before the arrival of European explorers. These groups are only a few of the hundreds that lived in North America. They were chosen to show some of the many different ways Native Americans lived.

The First Americans

Snowflakes drifted down from a dark-gray sky. They landed on a band of men, women, and children dressed in fur jackets and long leggings. On their backs, the people lugged wood for fires and hides for tents. All the men carried wooden spears. Frozen grass crunched under their thick boots as they crossed the vast plain.

This band of Asian hunters was tracking a herd of caribou (KAR uh boo), or wild deer. The caribou supplied meat for food, bones for tools, and skins for shelter and clothing. The people needed the caribou to live and so followed them everywhere. The caribou were leading them to a place no human had ever been—the North American continent.

All this took place between 15,000 and 35,000 years ago, during a time known as the Ice Age. Millions of tons of ocean water were locked in huge sheets of ice called glaciers. As a result, the ocean's water level dropped and left behind areas of high, dry ocean floor. One such area was the "land bridge" connecting Asia and Alaska. Over many centuries, groups of Asians crossed this bridge into Alaska.

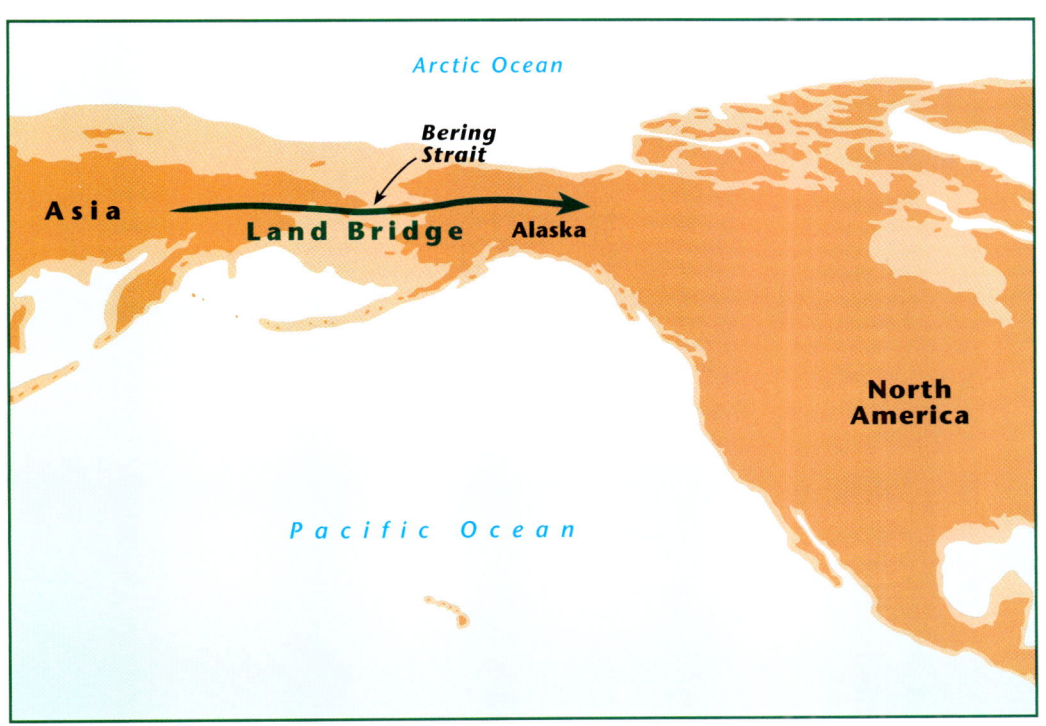

From Alaska, many of these groups continued south and east. Slowly, over thousands of years, their descendants spread across North America and into South America.

The Mighty Hunters

The prehistoric, or very early, hunters of North America lived in a land of plenty. Thousands of animals roamed the huge forests and great plains. The largest of these were furry elephants we call mammoths and mastodons.

At first, early Americans managed to kill these massive beasts with only wooden spears for

For thousands of years, a 1,000-mile-(1,600-kilometer-) wide strip of land joined what is now Asia and Alaska. Hunters crossed this land bridge for the first time between 15,000 and 35,000 years ago.

weapons. Of course, the hunters were often in danger. Some must have been hurt or killed by the sharp tusks and trampling feet of the giant elephants! As time went on, the hunters made stone points for their spears. These spears made it easier to kill even the biggest animals.

Herds of buffalo made easier game. Hunters trailed a herd until it neared the edge of a cliff. Then they threw spears, waved, and shouted to make the buffalo stampede over the edge. Scores of animals fell to their death at the bottom of the cliff. Then the hunters butchered the buffalo, ate some of the meat, and dried the rest for future use.

The First Farmers

Ten thousand years ago, North America was a different place than it had been centuries before. The climate was warmer. Most of the great glaciers had melted. The ocean had risen, and a water body now called the Bering Strait covered the land bridge between Asia and Alaska. The great mastodons and mammoths, which thrived during the Ice Age, were gone.

These changes meant a new way of life for many prehistoric Americans. Hunting was more difficult than it had been. People began to depend more on plants for food. They learned which fruits, nuts, seeds, and roots were good to eat.

Early Americans needed a lot of plant food to survive. So those who gathered plants for food lived in small groups. Even a small group of people soon ate up all the plant food in one place. Then they had to move on to another place to find more.

Some gatherers realized that new plants sprouted from seeds in the ground. So they began to sow seeds themselves. About 9,000 years ago, people in what is now Mexico became the first American farmers. They grew corn, beans, squash, red peppers, and avocados.

Over time, people in other places learned to plant crops and settled in permanent homes near their fields. As more and more people settled down, they built villages and towns.

The Mound Builders

Three thousand years ago, most people in what is now the United States and Canada were still hunters and gatherers. The exceptions were the mound builders. These people lived in villages, made pottery, and wove cloth from bark. They also built earthen mounds.

Most of the earliest mounds were dome-shaped. Their builders used them as graves for

The mound builders made their mounds by piling up earth to form a special shape. The Great Serpent Mound, shown above, may have taken hundreds of people and years to build. Located near Hillsboro, Ohio, the Great Serpent Mound resembles a huge snake and measures about 1/4 mile (0.4 kilometer) long.

These are the ruins of an Anasazi village. They are nearly a thousand years old. Called Cliff Palace, the ruins are in Mesa Verde National Park, Colorado.

their dead. Some of the mounds were shaped like animals and people. Later mounds looked like flat-topped pyramids. The mound builders put temples on top of these. Today you can still see thousands of mounds in the eastern half of the United States, but the people who built them were long gone when the Spanish came to America in the 1500's.

The Anasazi

About 900 years ago, the Anasazi lived in desert villages in the western part of North America. They had built hundreds of stone and clay houses nestled against the walls of cliffs. They wove cloth and baskets, made fine pottery, and grew corn and other crops in nearby fields.

Today, you can see the ruins of old cliff dwellings, standing silent and empty. Where did the Anasazi go? About 700 years ago, practically no rain fell in the western desert. This dry period went on for many years. Many experts think these cliff dwellers abandoned their homes because they could no longer grow crops. Others believe enemy groups may have driven the people away. No one knows for certain.

The Anasazi were the ancestors of the Hopi, Zuni, and other Pueblo Indians. These people still make houses out of stone and clay just as their ancestors did.

The People Called Native Americans

When Christopher Columbus reached the New World in 1492, he thought he was in a part of Asia known as the Indies. So he called the people he met "Indians."

As other Europeans arrived and met new groups of Americans, these Europeans called them Indians, too. However, each of these groups had a name they called themselves. Today, many of their descendants resent being mislabeled "Indians." They prefer the name of their own group or, when talking about all the groups, the names American Indians, Aboriginal or Native Peoples, First Nations, First Peoples, or similar terms.

Most Native Americans have descended from the hunters who came from Asia over the land bridge to Alaska. An exception is the Inuit. Their ancestors came from Asia long after the Ice Age ended. They probably crossed the Bering Strait in boats.

Some experts think that by 1492, up to 10 million or more Native Americans were living in North America.

The Inuit

People of the Arctic

The Inuit (IHN yoo iht) roamed the Arctic tundra in what is now Siberia, Alaska, northern Canada, and Greenland. The Arctic tundra is a vast, snow-covered plain surrounding the Arctic Ocean. The climate there is too cold and dry for farming or forests. Shrubs, mosses, tiny flowers, and grasslike plants called sedges grow there. Without crops or trees, Inuit had to hunt and fish to get food, clothing, shelter, tools, and fuel.

All Inuit spoke a similar language, used similar tools, worshiped similar spirits, and wore similar clothing. All Inuit lived in tents for the summer and built igloos, or shelters, for the winter. Canadian Inuit spent the winter in snowhouses. Other Inuit built winter houses of sod, whalebone, and wood.

In some parts of the Arctic, hundreds of people came together in the spring and fall to hunt caribou. During the rest of the year, the villages split up into families who went their own way to look for seal, fish, birds, and other animals. Another group of native Americans called the Aleuts lived to the west, on what are now Alaska's Aleutian Islands. Many Indian tribes lived south of the Inuit, including the Chipewyan, Hare, Koyukon, and Naskapi.

INUIT

North America

Life on the Arctic Tundra

Raven ran beside the sled, following the dogs over snowdrifts and around blocks of ice. Raven's father rode on the back of the sled. When he shouted, "Gee!" the lead dogs pulled the rest of the team to the right. When he shouted, "Haw!" the lead pair veered to the left.

If the leaders slowed down, two pointers nudged them from behind. A couple of puppies followed the pointers, learning about teamwork from their elders. Behind the puppies ran the wheel dogs. These were positioned right in front of the sled and pulled the most weight. They were the team's muscle.

Normally, Raven could not keep up with the team, but this morning the dogs were hauling most of the members of Raven's family and all of their possessions. Raven; his father; his mother; Strong Arm, his brother; Sea Gull, Strong Arm's wife; and Wolf, Raven's nephew, were headed for the Arctic coast. They planned to winter there, hunting walrus and seal.

Raven could just see a gray sliver of ocean on the horizon when his father stopped the sled. Raven, his mother, Strong Arm, and Sea Gull unloaded the sled while Wolf snuggled in the roomy hood of his mother's parka. His father scouted the area for the best site to build a snowhouse.

When the sled was empty, Strong Arm motioned for Raven to jump on. At Strong Arm's command, the team raced toward the ocean. He brought the dogs to a halt on the ice near the water's edge.

Strong Arm took a harpoon from the sled and unhitched Bear, his favorite lead dog. Raven jogged close behind Strong Arm, and the brothers and their dog went searching for breathing holes. These are holes in the ice where seals swimming below come up for air.

Bear soon found a hole and signaled to Strong Arm with a yelp. Strong Arm dipped his fingers inside a pouch hanging from his neck and pulled out a feather. He gently placed the feather on top of the water in the breathing hole. Then he lay on his belly with his harpoon in hand. Raven lay beside him. Together they waited for the feather to move. The moving feather would signal that a seal might be about to surface for air.

Meanwhile, back at camp, Raven's father had found just the right patch of snow that had hardened into ice. With a long, straight knife made of whalebone, he traced a large circle. From the ice inside the circle, he cut blocks 2 feet (61 centimeters) long, 20 inches (51 centimeters) high, and 4 inches (10 centimeters) thick. He arranged the blocks around the circle, leaving an opening for the doorway. Then he stacked each block on top of the one below, working his way up in one continuous coil. He slanted each layer inward, so it was closer to the center than the one beneath it, and formed a dome of clear ice for one of the snow blocks.

As Raven's father stacked the blocks, his wife and daughter-in-law covered the outer wall with soft snow. The snow filled the cracks between the blocks to keep out cold winds. Raven's father dug a tunnel leading to the entrance as a barrier against the cold. Then he carved a hole in the top of the block to let in fresh air.

Strong Arm and Raven returned with two seal carcasses slung over the sled. They ducked inside the snowhouse and found their father and the women sitting on a fur-covered platform. Heat from oil lamps made the inside too warm for outer clothing, so they wore only undergarments of caribou skin.

Raven's father hurriedly threw on his parka and boots and went out with his sons to butcher a seal. Raven's mother jumped up, filled a stone pot with snow, and placed it over a lamp to melt. Wolf napped through all the bustle while Sea Gull sat beside him, mending a rip in her parka with a bone needle and strip of sinew from a narwhal (NAHR hwuhl).

Outside the snowhouse, Strong Arm drove stakes into the snow. He unhitched the dogs and

tied them to the stakes. Then he buried one of the seals in the snow, storing it for another day.

His father dragged the other seal away from the dogs. Raven's mother then used a knife with a curved stone blade to peel away its hide. Next, she made pouches from parts of the hide. Then she chopped the blubber and meat into chunks and threw most of the chunks into the pouches. She tossed the leftovers to the dogs.

Raven carried the seal's ribs and the pouches of meat and blubber inside. His mother boiled the ribs, meat, and some of the blubber in the stone pot. She stored the rest of the blubber in the pouches. It would serve as fuel for the lamps or as food in case the men came home someday without a kill.

Raven gobbled three helpings of seal. Strong Arm teased him, saying his little brother was

beginning to look like a seal because he ate so much meat. Everyone laughed at the joke.

After eating, Raven and Strong Arm checked the team. They found the dogs sleeping under a blanket of windblown snow. Each one was curled up, its tail warming its nose.

The brothers rejoined the family as their father started telling about his grandfather, the celebrated angekok (ANG guh kahk). An angekok was a healer. "Grandfather's brother fell ill, so grandfather called on his helping spirit, the goose. Before my eyes, grandfather's neck grew long, and the fringe on his parka changed into feathers. He still looked human but like a goose at the same time.

"Grandfather flapped his arms, rose into the air, and glided over a nearby pond. There he spied a caribou that his brother had wounded but not killed. The hurt and confused caribou had stumbled into the water and drowned. Grandfather knew then that the sickness was great-uncle's punishment for making the animal suffer."

Raven never heard whether his great-great-uncle recovered. The boy drifted off before the story ended. In his dreams, he glided over the tundra on the wings of a raven.

Inuit Ways

The Arctic climate is so cold that clothing there can be a matter of life and death. Inuit women were constantly making and repairing snug-fitting shirts and trousers to keep out snow and to keep in warmth. In summer, this clothing was made of waterproof sealskin to keep the Inuit dry while they traveled and hunted by boat. In winter, the clothing was made of caribou skin, which was soft, lightweight, and had hollow hairs that trapped body heat.

The Inuit wore shirts and trousers with the fur facing their skin. Over that they wore jackets called parkas or anoraks (AH nuh rahks), with the fur facing out. Most Inuit made parkas of sealskin or caribou hide, but some made their parkas from fox, bear, or wolf fur. Special waterproof parkas worn only by men were pieced together from the skins of puffins, cormorants (KAWR muhr uhnts), and other water birds, or from walrus intestines.

Parkas featured tails in front and back. The tails in back hung longer for extra comfort when sitting on ice. Most parkas had hoods trimmed in long fur. This trim helped shed the crystals that formed when the wearer's breath turned to ice. Mothers' parkas had extra large hoods that they used to carry their babies in.

Most Inuit wore boots the year around. The uppers were made of caribou skin, and the soles of the tougher skin from seals. The soles were stuffed with moss to keep feet drier. Moss was also used in baby diapers to absorb wetness.

Mittens were a must on the tundra. Most were made of caribou hide, and they were often lined with woven grass, bear paws, or moss. Mittens not only kept hands warm but also prevented rope burn when hauling a seal or walrus out of the water after a kill.

While Inuit women sewed, Inuit men hunted. In summer, they harpooned seals and walruses from one-person

Inuit women sewed clothes while the men hunted. The Inuit made their clothing from the skins of animals. They preferred caribou skin as a material for clothing because it was lightweight and warm.

These women work beside a qulliq, *an Inuit lamp lit by whale or seal oil. Tending the qulliq was a very important task because the lamp provided light and heat for the family. It was customary that young women were not allowed to marry until they could tend a qulliq of their own.*

boats called kayaks (KY aks). Sometimes hunters used kayaks to drive a whale onto shore. Inuit made their kayaks by stretching seal or walrus hides over frames made of driftwood.

In winter, many Inuit took sleds to the coast to hunt sea mammals and to catch fish through holes in the ice. The Inuit shaped whalebones to attach to their sled runners and sometimes covered the runners with hides coated with frozen mud and moss to make the sleds glide more easily. Hunters often attached spikes to the soles of their boots to help them walk on the ice. They used poles to test the strength of the ice before sledding on it.

Different Inuit groups hunted caribou at different times of year. They also used different methods to kill the caribou. Some crept up on foot or in kayaks to get close enough to spear an animal or to shoot it with a bow and arrow. Some hid in snow pits and waited for caribou to wander near. Others drove whole herds of caribou into a corral or the sea.

The Inuit hunted many other land animals, including fish, whales, polar bears, foxes, hares, and birds. Sometimes the hunters caught the game with bolas (BOH luhz). These ropes had weights at both ends. A hunter threw a bola at an animal's legs, entangled them, and brought the animal to the ground.

Inuit knew how to play as well as work. In warm weather, they enjoyed outdoor games such as kickball, in which opposing teams tried to take control of a soft leather ball stuffed with caribou hair. They also played high kicks, in which they jumped up, kicked at a hanging object, and landed on two feet or in some other special way.

In the evenings, the Inuit liked to listen to stories. Storytellers often used ivory knives to draw scenes from their tales in the snow. When the smaller groups of Inuit gathered in a large group to hold a festival, they would build a giant igloo. Then they danced and sang to the music of drums.

Inuit men harpooned fish, seals, and walruses from kayaks. The Inuit usually fished with a three-pronged spear called a leister. *The Inuit also used a larger boat, called an* umiak, *for hunting walruses and whales.*

Target-and-pin Game

You Will Need

- cardboard tube from a toilet paper roll (target)
- nail or hole punch
- scissors
- transparent tape
- ruler
- string
- artist's small paintbrush (pin)

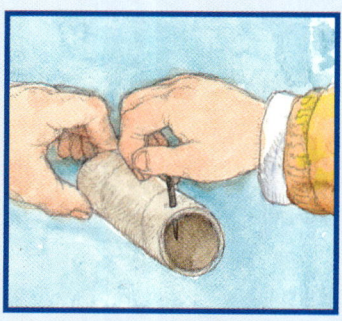

This is a popular Inuit game. It's not only fun, but it also helps build a sharp eye and a quick hand.

To play, an Inuk swings a tube target in the air and tries to "spear" it with a pin. Inuit carve the long pins and tube targets for this game from seal bones. They tie the playing pieces together with cord made of braided sinew. You can make a similar game with items from around your house.

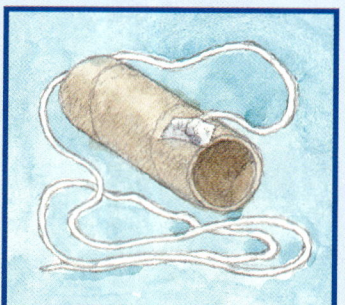

1 Use the nail to punch a hole in the cardboard tube near one end of the tube.

2 Cut 18 inches (46 centimeters) of string. Thread one end of the string through the punched hole and the end of the tube nearest it. Tie a knot. Secure the knot with tape.

3 Tie the other end of the string about one-third of the way along the length of the brush, measuring from the brush end. Secure the knot with tape. This is your "pin."

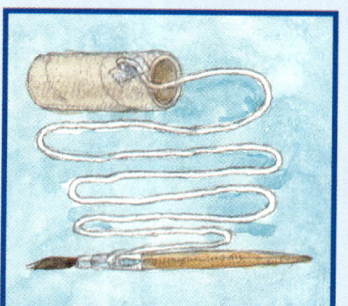

4 Hold the pin by the brush end and swing your target out and up. Try to spear the tube through its center with the pointed end of the brush. Keep trying and your hits will increase with practice.

Recovering the Past

Alix climbed off the single-engine plane onto the snow-covered runway. She pulled up her backpack, scanned the wooden buildings, and frowned. "What gives?" she said to herself.

"Alix? Welcome to Nunavut (NOO nuh voot). I am your guide, Jayko."

A black-haired man in an orange nylon jacket smiled broadly and offered his hand. Alix eyed him suspiciously.

"Where are the igloos?" she asked.

"It is summer. You can't build a decent snowhouse in summer. Besides, we do not make snowhouses anymore," Jayko answered "Except to show tourists. You are a student, aren't you, here to study the Inuit today?"

"I always thought you were called Eskimos," Alix said.

Jayko looked disappointed. "Eskimo is what other people named us. It means 'eater of raw meat,' and we consider the name an insult. We prefer Inuit, which in our language means 'real people.' "

"Sorry," Alix blushed. "I will make sure to call you an Inuit from here on in."

"Actually, one person is an Inuk, but you can call me Jayko."

"Well, I'm learning things already. Jayko, why did the Inuit give up their old lifestyle to settle in towns and live in ordinary houses?"

Jayko explained as he walked Alix to his snowmobile. "The change happened over time. It started when Europeans arrived. Vikings were the first to come. Then whalers, trappers, and fishing

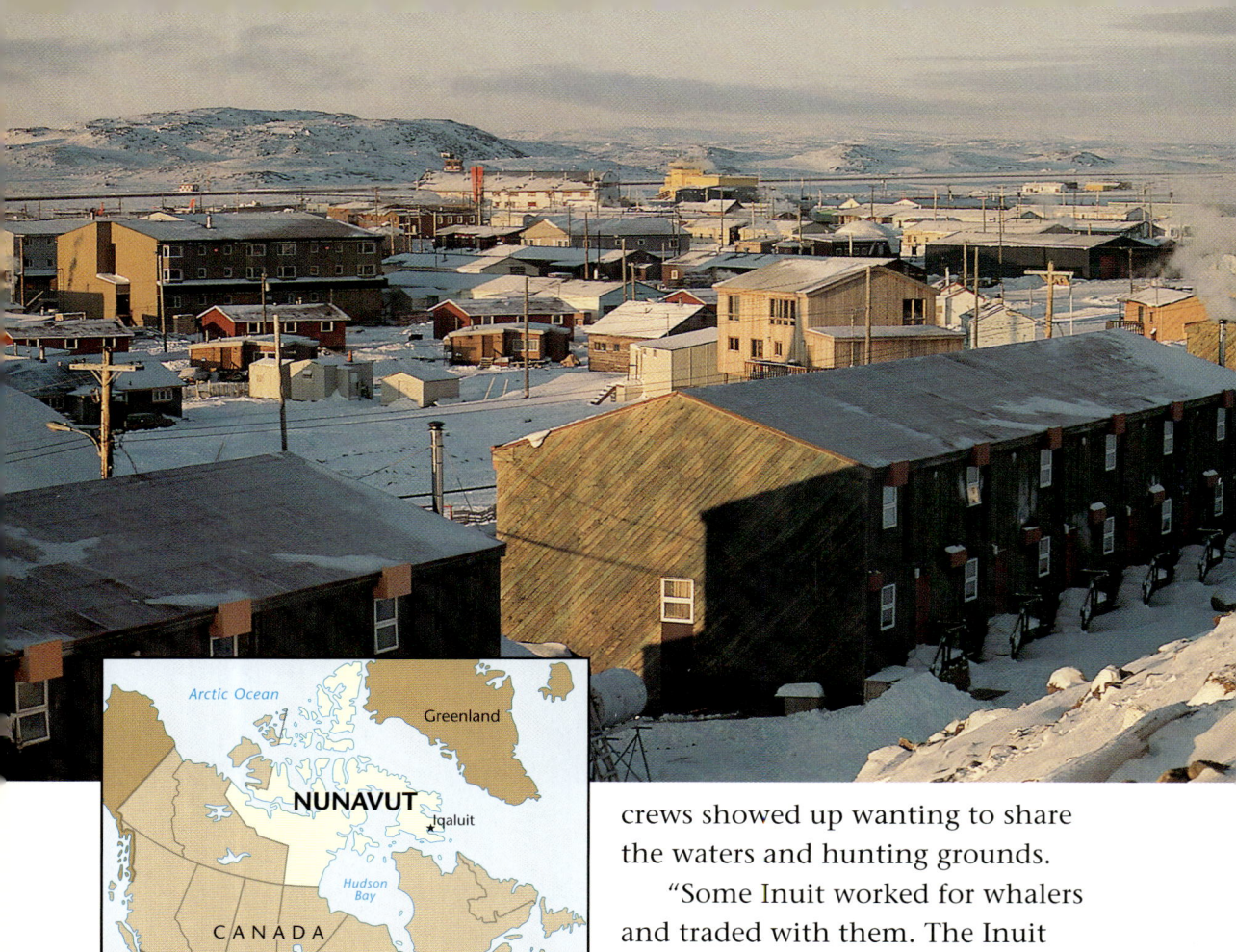

Iqaluit, Nunavut's capital and largest town, stands on Baffin Island, on the shores of Frobisher Bay. Iqaluit had long been used as a seasonal Inuit fishing camp when Europeans arrived in 1576. The town's name in Inuktitut, an Inuit language, means place of fish.

crews showed up wanting to share the waters and hunting grounds.

"Some Inuit worked for whalers and traded with them. The Inuit received firearms, ammunition, wood, iron, and other European goods. Unfortunately, European diseases often came with the whalers and traders. These diseases, such as tuberculosis and smallpox, completely wiped out large groups of Inuit. When such large groups of Inuit died, their ways of living also died, because there was nobody left to pass along their traditions and customs.

"The groups of Inuit that survived traded animal skins and furs with Europeans for their beads, firearms, and metal knives. Many Inuit grew to depend on European goods. Eventually, the Inuit stopped making their own tools and passing down that knowledge to the next generation. They forgot how to make their own tools. To get the goods they needed, many Inuit began to trap animals for their furs alone, and the game in some areas disappeared.

"Slowly, the Inuit traditions continued to be lost. When missionaries came, they told Inuit children to place their faith in Christianity rather than guardian spirits. The Inuit stopped believing in gods that governed the sea, wind, and weather.

"Governments played a part, too. They changed the spelling of Inuit names to make them more like European names. In 1969, the Canadian government passed a law demanding that Inuit use last names, which they had never used before. Today, many Inuit are working to change the spellings of their names that were recorded in the 1970's so they are more true to the Inuit language.

"Hunting and fishing are still important to the Inuit economy, but we use rifles instead of spears, snowmobiles instead of dogsleds, and motorboats instead of kayaks. Many traditions are being preserved as works of art, though. For example, Simon Tookoome and other artists have re-created guardian spirits and drum dances in their prints and drawings. Inuit craftworkers also carve dolls and tiny animals out of bone and soapstone and sell them as sculptures.

"The Inuit population almost doubled between 1950 and 1970, and it continues to grow rapidly. This growth has resulted chiefly from better medical care and living conditions.

"In 1999, a territory called Nunavut was formed for many of Canada's Inuit. It covers an area the size of Mexico, so we now have plenty of rich resources to develop. We will use some of those riches to preserve our Inuit past. We plan to use the rest to build a better future."

Many Inuit artists belong to organizations called collectives, *which collect the artwork of their members and sell it throughout the world. Handicrafts, such as this ivory polar bear by a northwest Greenland sculptor and this soapstone carving of a mother and baby by a Nunavut artist, have become increasingly popular.*

The Ojibwa

People of the Great Lakes

The Ojibwa (oh JIHB wah *or* oh JIHB way), also called Chippewa, were one of the largest Indian tribes north of Mexico. The name they gave themselves was Anishinabe (ah nihsh ih NAH bay), meaning "First People." They lived in what are now Michigan's Upper Peninsula, northern Wisconsin and Minnesota, and part of Ontario, Canada.

Many rivers ran through the land of the Ojibwa. Many small lakes, as well as the largest of the Great Lakes, now called Lakes Superior and Huron, also lay in their country. The Ojibwa traveled in canoes made of birchbark. In winter, they traveled over the frozen water by foot. They moved about their land according to the seasons.

Towering oak, birch, and maple trees covered their land. The Ojibwa lived in the forest in camps of from 50 to a few hundred people. Each camp hunted and gathered plants in its own part of the forest. Each camp had its own leader. When a leader died, his son became the new leader.

Tribes to the south of the Ojibwa were the Menominee, Sauk, and Winnebago. To the west lived the Dakota, or Sioux, people. The Cree were to the north.

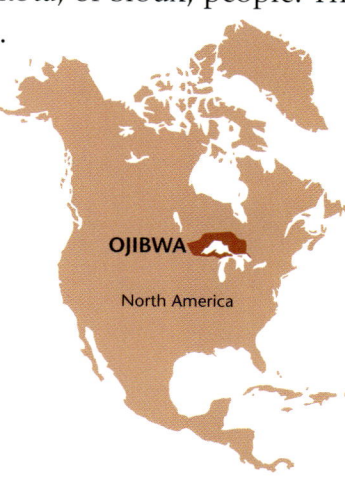

OJIBWA

North America

Life in the Forest

Grasshopper walked through the forest with her family and the other people who belonged to the camp led by Old Man. It was a bright, hot summer day, but the forest was cool and dim. The leafy branches of the trees shut out much of the sunlight.

There were about 200 people in Old Man's camp—men, women, and children of all ages. They were part of the great tribe of Anishinabe or "First People." There were many camps of the First People in other parts of the forest.

The people of Old Man's camp walked quietly, one behind another. By making only a narrow path, the people let the forest and the animals know that they were only passing through, not claiming ownership. The forest belonged to the animals, not to the Anishinabe.

Yet the forest was home to Grasshopper and her people. They moved about it freely, going from place to place. Because they depended upon the forest, the rivers, and the lakes for all their food, they settled in a different place each season. They went wherever the hunting or fishing was best, or where wild plant food had become ripe enough to eat.

Now they were on their way to a part of the forest where they knew wild blueberries grew. They went there at about the same time every year. In fact, they called this time of year "Blueberry Moon." Grasshopper licked her lips at the thought of sweet blueberries.

"Grasshopper" was not her real name. It was a nickname her father had given her. Her real name was Coming-Over-the-Hill, but no one ever called her by this name. Grasshopper had been given her real name when she was a tiny baby. An old woman who had dreamed of deer coming over a hill had given it to her. A person's real name was a very important thing that must be kept secret. A real name loses its power if it is spoken too much.

Just then, one of Grasshopper's little brothers strayed off the path, into the woods. One of her fathers called him back, sharply. The man who called was not her real father. He was one of her father's brothers, but Grasshopper called both of her father's brothers "father." She also called their wives "mother," and she called their children brothers and sisters. All of these people, together with her father's father and mother were Grasshopper's family.

The family had no last name, but all the men belonged to a group of related people who called themselves the Bear clan, or Bear group. All of the children belonged to the Bear clan because their fathers did. The mothers belonged to other clans, for people of the same clan never married one another. When, in time, Grasshopper married, she would join another family. Her children would belong to the clan of the man she married, such as Wolf, or Goose, but Grasshopper would always belong to the Bear clan.

Grasshopper wiggled her shoulders to ease the weight of the small bundle on her back. Everyone in the camp carried a bundle. Whenever they moved to another place, they took all their

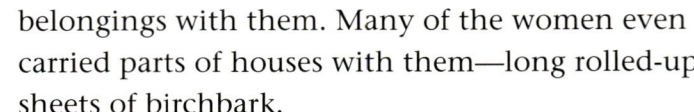

belongings with them. Many of the women even carried parts of houses with them—long rolled-up sheets of birchbark.

The camp reached the berry patch in late afternoon. Everyone went right to work.

The women began to put up the houses. A number of dome-shaped frames made of trimmed tree branches already stood in the small clearing near the berry patch. These frames had been built years before. Now the women unrolled the sheets of birchbark they had carried. They used these to cover the frames. While the camp stayed at the berry patch, the people would sleep in these birchbark-covered wigwams.

The men and older boys went hunting. Grasshopper and many of the other children went to pick berries. They put the berries into square buckets made of birchbark.

Soon, the setting sun sent orange shafts of light slanting through the trees.

Shadows began to fill the forest. Some of the women started fires.

To start a fire, they twirled a hard, pointed wooden stick between their hands. The point of the stick pressed against a piece of soft bark. As the point spun, it ground some of the bark to powder. The spinning end of the pointed stick and the powdered bark got hotter and hotter. Finally, the powdered bark caught fire. Quickly, the women fed the fire with twigs and leaves.

The men and boys returned from their hunt. They had managed to kill only a few birds, but they had set a number of traps. They also had found a trail used by deer. Tomorrow, they would have more time, and probably better luck, but for now, each family had a small supply of dried meat and fish—and there were plenty of blueberries.

Night fell. The cluster of fires twinkled in the darkness. Around each fire sat a family group. At Grasshopper's family fire, all of the children sat silent and wide-eyed as Grandmother told stories.

She told of the Windigo, the giant who eats people. She spoke of Nhenebush, the creature that looks like a coyote and goes about doing harm to people. She also told tales of Hare, the great spirit that had given the First People fire and other things.

One by one, as the fires died down, the families went into their wigwams to sleep. Grasshopper curled up with her brothers and sisters on mats made of dried rushes. The last thing she heard before she fell asleep was the sound of an owl hooting in the blackness of the forest.

The people of the camp would stay at the berry patch for several weeks. They would pick all

the berries they could. Many berries would be eaten, but many would be dried for later use. Then the people would move to the shore of the great lake. There they gathered wild rice each year. They would stay there for a time, gathering the rice and drying it. Then they would move on to another part of the woods.

Grasshopper's world was the great lake and the forest that surrounded it. The wigwams in the woods or by the lake were not homes. They were just places to sleep. The forest was Grasshopper's home. Everything she needed came from the forest or the lake.

The Ojibwa

Ojibwa Ways

If you had been an Ojibwa child of long ago, you would have worn clothes made from the skin of a fawn, a young deer. Your parents would have clothes made from the skins of deer, elk, or moose. The Ojibwa, like all Woodland Indians, made their clothes from the skins of animals.

Your mother would have done all the work to prepare the skins. This was a long and hard task. If you had been a teen-aged girl, you would have helped.

First, your mother would soak the skin in water for several days. Then, after wringing it out, she would use a sharp-edged bone to scrape off all the flesh. With a stone blade, should would then remove the hair.

Next, she would soak the skin overnight in water in which deer brains had been boiled. Then she would scrape and stretch the skin again and again to smooth out the bumps and flaws and make it soft. Finally, she would tan the skin by smoking it over glowing embers. This would color the skin and protect it from insects and worms. After this tanning, the skin would be soft as silk and ready to be made into clothes.

Ojibwa women prepared the animal skins from which they made clothes for the family. To take off the hair and flesh, a damp skin was put over a log and scraped with sharp tools. The skin was then stretched tight on a frame and scraped again to make it smooth and soft.

In summer, an Ojibwa man often wore only a breechclout. This was a narrow band of deerskin that passed between the legs and looped over the front and rear of a leather belt. He might also wear leggings. Each legging was separate and was tied to the belt holding the breechclout.

Most of the time, you and your family would sleep in a dome-shaped lodge called a wigwam. A wigwam was a simple framework of poles covered with sheets of birchbark or mats made of cattails. At the center of your wigwam there would be a pit where a fire could be made for light and cooking. Your only furniture would be mats made of dried, woven plant stems. You would sit as well as sleep on these mats.

In the cold winter months you would live in a larger house with three or four other families. This kind of house, called a lodge, looked like a peaked roof sitting on the ground. It was made by placing two rows of poles in the ground, slanted so the tops met and supported a long pole at the peak. The poles were covered with bark sheets or mats.

If you had been an older boy, you would have spent most of your time with the men, hunting, trapping, and fishing for food. You would shoot moose, elk, and deer with arrows that had tiny hooks on them. You would shoot birds with blunt arrows that stunned them.

To catch bears, you would use a trap called a deadfall. Such a trap drops a heavy log on the bear, pinning the animal down. You would catch rabbits, foxes, and even deer in a trap called a snare. This kind of trap has a noose that tightens around the animal.

Ojibwa women trimmed and peeled the poles used to make the frame for a wigwam. The men drove poles into the ground and then bent and held them while the women tied them. The women covered the frame with sheets of birchbark or mats made of cattails.

The Ojibwa caught bears in a trap called a deadfall. When the bear took the bait, the post holding up the crosspiece moved and the heavy log fell on the animal.

The Ojibwa   37

In warm weather, you might help the men catch fish in big nets or in wide traps called weirs, both made of woven bark. In winter, you would fish through a hole in the ice.

In early spring, your camp would go to a place where there were many sugar maple trees. Your father would make cuts in the tree trunks to allow the sap to drip into birchbark buckets. Then your mother would boil the sap down into maple sugar.

During the summer, you might help the women and other children pick berries. Then, in late August or early September, in the time called Turning-of-Leaves-Moon, you would move to the lake. There, your parents would gather wild rice, one of your most important foods.

The Ojibwa harvested wild rice from their birchbark canoes. One person guided the canoe. Others bent down the stalks of rice and beat them lightly to knock the ripe kernels into the canoe. Kernels that fell into the water would take root and grow into new plants.

How Hare Brought Fire Home

An Ojibwa Legend

The great god Hare was born to a young woman who lived with her mother in a wigwam in the forest. Hare's father was the west wind. When Hare was born, his mother died. His grandmother brought him up.

One day, Hare said to his grandmother, "Do any people live near us?"

"Yes," said his grandmother. "There are people living on the far shore of the lake."

"Do these people across the lake have fire?" asked Hare.

"Indeed they do," she replied.

"Then I shall go and bring back some fire for us," he said.

"Oh, you cannot do that," said his grandmother. "They keep a careful watch over their fire. There is an old man who sits at home by the fire all day long, mending a fishing net. He has two daughters who often go outside, but he never leaves the fire."

"Nevertheless, I will go," declared Hare.

When Hare came to the lake, he stood on the shore and said, "I wish this lake to freeze. I wish it to become as thick as the birchbark covering of a wigwam. Let this happen." Then the lake froze.

"Now," said Hare, "let me become a small rabbit." Then he became a small rabbit.

Then Hare started out onto the ice, which easily held his light weight. He crossed over to the far shore. There, he found a place where the water was not frozen. Hare lay down in the water and said, "Let a young girl now come to get water. Let her take me home for a pet."

Almost at once, a young girl carrying a dipper came down to the water. When she saw the little rabbit, she lifted him out of the water. Tucking him inside her robe to keep him warm, she went home.

When they went into the wigwam, Hare saw the old man sitting by the fire, mending a net. The girl who had found Hare went over to her sister and whispered, "Look at the cute little rabbit I found. Isn't he nice? I hope you like him as much as I do."

Her sister whispered back, "Father will be

angry if he sees it. Wait and see."

But the girl who had found Hare took him out of her robe and put him down by the fire to dry. He looked so funny that the two girls began to giggle.

"Why are you making so much noise?" asked the old man, their father.

"Look at this cute little rabbit I found," said the girl.

"Beware!" exclaimed her father. "Have you never heard of the spirits? Perhaps this is one! Go put it back where you found it. You were wrong to bring it here!"

The girl objected, "Oh, I like this funny little rabbit so much! How could a little bunny be a spirit?"

"Listen to what I tell you!" said her father, angrily. "I am older than you, and I know more about such things."

Then Hare thought to himself, "Let a spark from the fire now fall upon me." That is what

happened. A spark fell upon him and his fur caught fire. Instantly, Hare sprang up and dashed out of the wigwam.

"You see!" cried the girls' father. "Why did you not listen to me? I tell you, that rabbit is a spirit that has come to steal fire from us!" Angrily, the old man got up and ran after Hare.

Hare scurried to the lake and began to run across the frozen water. The man and his daughters saw they would never be able to catch him. All they could do was stand and watch him until he was out of sight.

Hare sped across the lake, his fur burning. Soon, he saw his grandmother's wigwam ahead. "Grandmother!" he called. "Rub this fire off me, for I am burning up!"

His grandmother rubbed the fire off him with some sticks. At once, the sticks began to burn. That is how the spirit Hare brought fire to the land of the Ojibwa.

What Happened to My People

"At one time, long ago, my people—the Ojibwa—were Indians who lived in the northernmost parts around the Great Lakes." As the old man spoke, he looked out across Lake Superior to the forest along the shores. "One of your people told of our way of life, our beliefs, and our legends in a long poem, *The Song of Hiawatha*."

American Indian Movement (AIM) activists Dennis Banks, left, and Clyde Bellecourt beat a drum and chant during a protest rally at the Pine Ridge Reservation in South Dakota.

The old man paused, then went on. "That way of life was long ago. It was a dream, and now the dream is gone. For us, it ended the day we first met the whites. These people—they were French—were like us in some ways and very different in other ways. They wanted furs, and we had furs. They had all kinds of things we needed—but most of all, they had guns.

"The Ojibwa have always been the bravest of warriors. Always we were ready to fight to keep what was ours." His eyes flashed. "With guns, we could keep the wild rice fields, and we did. We drove the Dakota, or Sioux, people onto the plains to the west. We drove our southern neighbors further south, and when the mighty tribes of the Iroquois came at us from the east, we pushed them back.

"But in the late 1700's, white settlers came in greater and greater numbers. We had land. They wanted it. They took it."

Then, for a moment, the old man stood straight and tall. His voice was proud as he spoke. "We held them back at first and won great victories. Many tribes banded together under the Miami war chief Little Turtle and the great Shawnee

leader Tecumseh. At a place called Fallen Timbers, in what is now Ohio, the Shawnee chief Blue Jacket attacked an American force under Major General 'Mad Anthony' Wayne. The Americans were too much for us. We thought our British friends would help us, but when we fell back to one of their forts, they would not even open the gates."

The old man sat down cross-legged on the ground. "In the mid-1800's, the Ojibwa living in the United States signed a series of treaties with the government. We gave up our land and settled in places called reservations. Some of us stayed on the reservations, but many others moved to cities.

"In 1968, three city Ojibwa—Dennis Banks, Clyde Bellecourt, and George Mitchell—founded the American Indian Movement (AIM). AIM protested how state and national governments broke their promises to Native Americans and drew attention to the hardships of people living on reservations.

"Today, there are about 106,000 Ojibwa. We live mainly in Michigan, Wisconsin, Minnesota, and North Dakota, and in Ontario and Manitoba, Canada. Many of us make our living by hunting, lumbering, or harvesting rice. We harvest almost all the wild rice sold in the United States. Other Ojibwa work as teachers, lawyers, and doctors. Some are gifted artists.

"So, you see, we have learned to live in the modern world. But we also are trying to keep what was best from our past."

Winona LaDuke

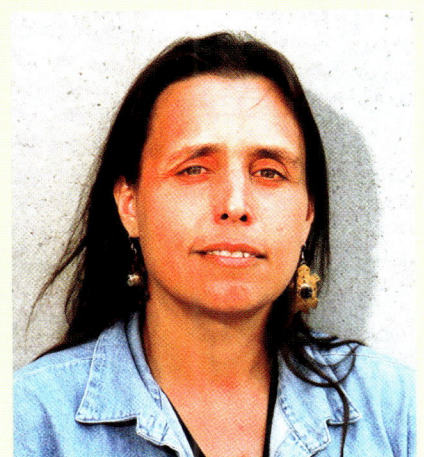

Winona LaDuke, of Anishinabe and Jewish heritage, was born in 1959 in East Los Angeles. She is a leading activist for Native American and environmental issues.

• She became involved in Native American environmental issues while attending Harvard University. After graduating, she moved to White Earth Reservation in Minnesota.

• In 1995, she was named one of Time *magazine's "50 Leaders of the Future."*

• LaDuke ran as Ralph Nader's vice presidential running mate for the Green Party in the 2000 presidential election.

The Ojibwa  **45**

The Iroquois

People of the Northeast Longhouse

The Iroquois lived in most of what is now New York State. Their villages stood in clearings in the forest that covered the land. They had large houses, called longhouses, in which a number of families lived. The men hunted, fished, and made war. The women grew corn, beans, and squash outside the village.

Five tribes—the Mohawk, Oneida, Onondaga, Cayuga, and Seneca—lived in this area. All of them spoke the same basic language and lived in much the same way. Long ago, these five tribes had joined together to form a strong group. They called their group by a name meaning "we are of the longhouse."

Their enemies, the Algonquin Indians, called all the people of the longhouse by a name meaning "snakes." To French explorers, the Algonquin word sounded like *Iroquois* (IHR uh kwoy). We still know them by this name.

IROQUOIS

North America

Life in a Mohawk Village

It was about noon. For the people living in the longhouse, it was time for the main meal of the day. The men had just eaten and left. Now the women and children would have their turn.

Bright Sky sat by the fire, gobbling the corn soup his mother had given him. He ate with a large wooden spoon that had a deep bowl. The soup contained the only meat he would have during the day. His evening meal would probably be corn cakes and nuts.

Bright Sky's home, the longhouse, was like a long hall. There were a dozen such longhouses in the village. This was a village of the people who called themselves "The People of the Place of Flint." Their enemies, who feared and hated them, called them "People Eaters."

The People of the Place of Flint were one of the five tribes that had joined together to form a group called the Five Nations, or the League of the Iroquois. These five tribes—the Seneca, Cayuga, Onondaga, Oneida, and Mohawk— thought of themselves as living in one great longhouse.

The Seneca, in the west, were "Keepers of the Western Door" of the longhouse. In the center were the Onondaga, "Keepers of the Fire and the Wampum Belts." The Mohawk were "Keepers of the Eastern Door."

As Bright Sky sat eating in the longhouse, he thought of these things. He also thought of his family. He, his baby sister, and his mother and father were a "fireside family." All the other people living in the longhouse made up his "longhouse family." It was this group that was most important to him.

The head of the longhouse family was his grandmother—his mother's mother. She was the oldest woman of the family. Grandmother had two daughters living in the longhouse. Grandmother's sister had a daughter and a son who lived there. All three of the daughters were married and had children. All of these people made up Bright Sky's longhouse family. He called all the children his brothers and sisters.

Bright Sky's grandfather and father, as well as the husbands of the other women, lived in the longhouse, but they were not part of this longhouse family. They belonged to other longhouse families—the longhouses where their mothers and sisters lived. When Bright Sky grew up and married, he would move into the longhouse of his wife's family. Even so, he would still belong to his mother's family in the longhouse where he now lived.

Bright Sky began to wonder what his father was doing now. Many suns ago, his father and many of the other men had gone off with a war party. They had gone to raid a village of the enemy people they called Atirontaks, meaning "Tree-Bark Eaters."

The Iroquois

Bright Sky remembered the excitement as the war party formed. The loud whoops of Fish Carrier, who was war chief, told the village that war had been decided on. Fish Carrier went to the war post, a wooden post that stood near the center of the village. He struck the post with a red-painted hatchet. The hatchet was still there, its stone head stuck in the post. It would stay there until the men returned.

Fish Carrier then began to dance. One by one, most of the young men joined in the dance. This showed their willingness to go to war. Quickly, the women brought food for the warriors—dried corn that had been ground to powder and mixed with maple sugar. The men loaded the food into bearskin pouches, seized their bows, hatchets, and clubs, and left at once. That had been days ago.

Bright Sky wished he were old enough to go with the war party! War was the way a man of the People of the Place of Flint proved himself worthy. It was the way to gain honor and glory. Only two moons ago, in early summer, another war party had gone on a raid. They had brought back many prisoners. All warriors had been praised and honored! Bright Sky remembered just what had happened.

First, the villagers tested the prisoners, all young men, for bravery. All the men and women formed two lines, facing each other. Everyone held a stout stick or a thorny branch. One by one, the prisoners ran between the lines. The men and women struck at them with their sticks and branches. The prisoners were soon bruised and bloody.

Two prisoners did not make it to the end. They staggered and fell. The village men killed them both, for they were not worthy.

The prisoners who did make it to the end of the line were worthy. They were adopted into the tribe. They were given to women whose husbands or sons had died of sickness or been killed in war. They would take the places of those men. They would be warriors and hunters of the People of the Place of Flint.

One woman, whose husband had not come back with the rest of the war party, was impressed with the bravery of her newly adopted man. And so, she decided he should be put to death as a sacrifice to her people. He was burned all over his body with torches, beaten, and hurt in other ways until he was near death. Then he was killed, cooked, and eaten. In this way everyone gained a share of the man's courage.

When the war party returned, it would be autumn. Winter was approaching. Then it would be time for making things that were needed— bows, paddles, snowshoes, bowls, and cups. The men made these things out of wood. The women made clay pots, woven baskets, and clothing.

Bright Sky suddenly realized that his mother was speaking to him. Most of the women and children had finished eating. They were leaving the longhouse.

His mother and the other women were going to their patches of farmland outside the village. The farms, like the longhouses, belonged to the women. His mother had his baby sister strapped to her back in a cradleboard. When she reached her field, she would hang the cradleboard from a tree branch while she worked. A year ago, Bright Sky would have gone with his mother. Then, he had had to help with the corn, beans, and squash.

The Iroquois

Now he was eight summers old. It was time for him to learn the ways of a man. The forest was the place of the man.

With some of his brothers, Bright Sky started toward the woods. Boys his age and older spent their days in the forest. There they learned the ways of the animals and how to hunt. They also played war and other games. When Bright Sky was a man, the forest would be his second home. Hunting and war would be the most important things in his life.

*I*roquois Ways

The Iroquois built their villages deep in the woods. They always selected a place close to a stream, so that they would have water for drinking and cooking. They cut and burned the trees around the village so that they could grow crops. Thus there was blue sky above an Iroquois village. The sun shone down on the houses, but only a short distance away, on all sides, was the green, dark forest.

Each village was surrounded by a high wall of logs. The logs were stuck upright in the ground, side by side, and the tops sharpened to a point. The village farmland lay just outside the wall.

An Iroquois village might have four or five houses, or dozens. These houses, called longhouses, looked like long, narrow barns. The walls were made of thick sheets of elm bark, fastened to poles stuck in the ground. Each roof was also made of elm bark. The men built the houses, but the houses belonged to the women.

As many as 10 families—about 50 people— lived in a longhouse. Each family had a small, open "room." These rooms were on each side of the house. Cooking fires, shared by the two families across from each other, glowed in the fire pits at mealtime.

Both men and women wore long deerskin tops and moccasins. These were often decorated with dyed porcupine quills. The men also wore leather breechclouts and leather leggings. The women wore long skirts. In very cold weather, the women also often put on short leggings that reached from just below their knees to their ankles.

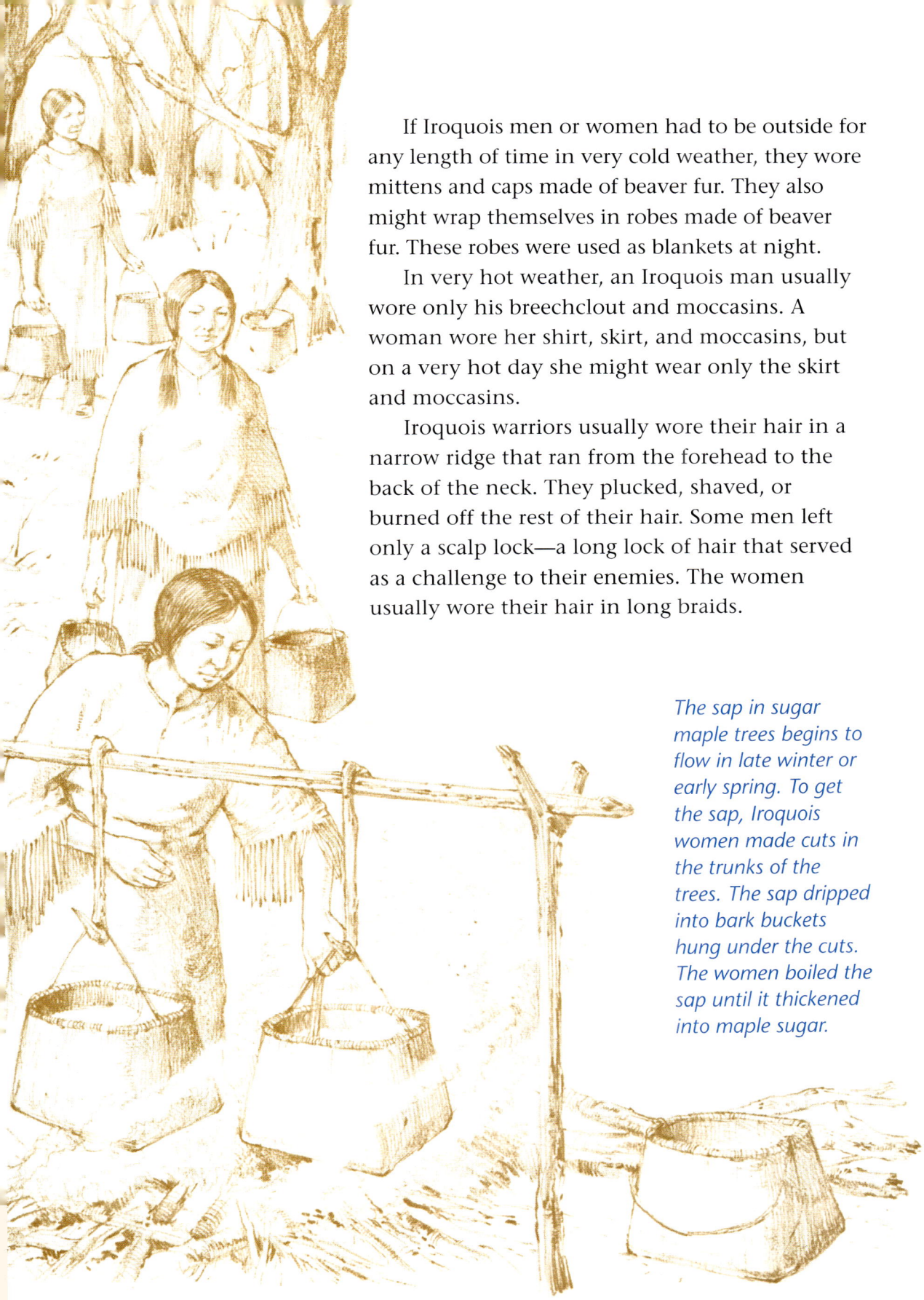

If Iroquois men or women had to be outside for any length of time in very cold weather, they wore mittens and caps made of beaver fur. They also might wrap themselves in robes made of beaver fur. These robes were used as blankets at night.

In very hot weather, an Iroquois man usually wore only his breechclout and moccasins. A woman wore her shirt, skirt, and moccasins, but on a very hot day she might wear only the skirt and moccasins.

Iroquois warriors usually wore their hair in a narrow ridge that ran from the forehead to the back of the neck. They plucked, shaved, or burned off the rest of their hair. Some men left only a scalp lock—a long lock of hair that served as a challenge to their enemies. The women usually wore their hair in long braids.

The sap in sugar maple trees begins to flow in late winter or early spring. To get the sap, Iroquois women made cuts in the trunks of the trees. The sap dripped into bark buckets hung under the cuts. The women boiled the sap until it thickened into maple sugar.

An Iroquois longhouse was smoky, drafty, and full of people. A row of fire pits ran down the middle. Narrow slits in the roof let out some smoke.

If you had been an Iroquois child, your favorite dish might have been a soup made out of corn, beans—and chopped bear meat!

For food, the Iroquois depended on the animals of the forest and the crops grown on the farmland outside the village. Their main foods, which they called "the three sisters," were corn, beans, and squash.

Corn was used in a great many ways. Green corn was boiled, roasted, or made into soup. Ripe corn was dried and pounded into a coarse powder. This corn meal was baked into cakes or used to make a kind of mushy pudding. The Iroquois often boiled corn and beans together to make what we call succotash. This is a dish many people enjoy today. The Iroquois also ate another kind of corn that is popular now—popcorn—but they did not put butter and salt on it.

Iroquois women cut pumpkins and other kinds of squashes into long strips. After drying the strips with heat, they stored them away for winter. They hung up ears of corn to dry, then stored them in bark containers for use in the winter.

Women and girls also searched in the forest for wild plant food. The Iroquois enjoyed eating mushrooms, berries, and nuts. They ate them raw or cooked and mixed them with other foods. They also ate boiled dandelions and other leafy plants.

The Iroquois usually roasted meat. Parts of animals that did not have much meat on them—such as bear's head—were often skinned, cut up, and added to soup. Strips of deer meat and bear meat were smoked and stored away for winter.

False Face Medicine

The sick man lay in the longhouse. His wife knelt beside him.

Suddenly, from outside the longhouse, came the clatter of many rattles. There were grunts and strange cries outside the door. Then, a group of people in frightening masks came creeping in.

The sick man smiled feebly. The False Faces had come! Now, he would be well!

The Iroquois believed that certain kinds of sickness were caused by spirits, and could be cured only by spirits. So when the Iroquois got sick, they often sent for the False Faces to come and help them get well. The False Faces were men who belonged to a special club, or society. The masks they wore represented the faces of powerful spirits that could cure disease.

The society was made up of men who

had once been sick themselves. While sick, they had dreamed of frightening faces. This meant the spirits were communicating with them. When the men were well, they became members of the society and masks were made for them.

Each mask was carved on the trunk of a live tree, then removed. A mask carved in the morning was painted red. A mask carved in the afternoon was painted black. If the carving took both morning and afternoon, the mask was painted red and black. Horsehair and brass eye plates were added. The masks were treated with great respect. They were often rubbed with oil and sprinkled with tobacco.

Wearing their masks, the False Faces went to the house of a sick person. They shook their turtle-shell rattles over the sick one and sprinkled him or her with tobacco ashes. They sang in high, squawky voices, in a strange "made-up" language even they did not understand. It was thought that this was how the spirits sounded.

After the False Faces visited a sick person, they were given gifts of tobacco and corn meal pudding. These gifts were not for them. They were for the spirits that the carved masks represented.

While the False Faces wore their masks, they believed that the spirit of the mask was with them. They believed this gave them the power to cure sickness. The sick person believed this, too, very strongly. A visit by the False Faces often made a sick Iroquois feel much better, which would help him or her to get well.

The Iroquois do not like to show the False Face masks outside of their community because they are considered sacred, and the Iroquois want to respect and preserve their special culture.

An Iroquois Game You Can Play

The Iroquois enjoyed a game they called "the dish." This game was played with six wild plum pits ground down smooth and flat on each side. The Iroquois painted the pits black on one side and white on the other.

To play the game, three or four people made a "pot" by putting 100 dried beans into a bowl. The plum pits were placed in another bowl. Each player took turns shaking the bowl and throwing the pits into the air so that they turned over several times.

If the pits landed on the ground so that three or four were black or white, the player passed the pits and bowl to the next player. But if the pits came down so that five or six were all one color, the player was a winner.

For five pits of the same color, the player got to take 5 beans from the pot. If all six pits were the same color, the player took 20 beans. The player also took another turn if he or she won any beans. When all the beans were gone from the pot, the player with the most beans won.

You can play this Iroquois game. Instead of wild plum pits, use six large buttons. Paint the buttons, or mark them, so that one side is different from the other. For the pot, use beans, as the Iroquois did, or peanuts, or anything similar.

You will need

- 6 large buttons
- 100 beans or peanuts
- 2 bowls
- markers or paint to mark the buttons

Steam Baths

The Iroquois, like many of the Indians of North America, enjoyed taking steam baths.

An Iroquois village was always near a stream or river. At the edge of the stream, the people built a small, dome-shaped hut for use as a sweat lodge. This hut was made of a framework of branches covered with sheets of elm bark. It was just big enough for two or three people to sit in.

When the Iroquois wanted to take a steam bath, they built a large fire next to the hut. Then they dropped 10 or 20 round stones into the fire. When the stones were red hot, the people used forked sticks to pull them into a pit in the center of the bathhouse. Then the entrance to the hut was closed.

Inside the hut was a bucket made out of bark and filled with water. The Indians poured the water over the pile of red-hot stones. Clouds of steam filled the hut. The air grew thick and very hot. The people soon began to sweat. When they could no longer stand the heat and thick steam, they burst out of the bathhouse and plunged into the cool water of the stream.

For Iroquois and other Indians, the baths were a sort of religious ceremony. As they bathed, people prayed to the spirits they believed in. The Indians felt they made themselves pure by sweating. Warriors took a steam bath before going to war. Hunters often took a steam bath before a hunt. Indians also believed that steam baths kept them healthy.

How the Bow and Arrow Were Invented

An Iroquois Legend

One day, long ago, a young Iroquois brave named Ohgweluhndoe went into the forest to hunt bear. He carried a long spear with a point made of flint. This was the only kind of weapon the Iroquois had in those days.

Ohgweluhndoe traveled far through the woods, but he did not find any tracks or signs of bear. Then a thought came to him. Perhaps he would find a bear in the thick part of the forest in a place where he knew there were many grapes. It was autumn, the Moon of Falling Leaves. The grapes would be ripe and juicy. Surely, a bear would go there to eat the grapes.

The young warrior headed for the place of the grapes. When he reached it, sure enough, there was Oh-gwa-li, the bear, eating grapes. As he swallowed the grapes, he gave little squeals of pleasure, for Oh-gwa-li loves to eat grapes.

Ohgweluhndoe crept up quietly behind the big, black animal and raised his spear, but at that instant his foot slipped. He fell flat on his back.

The startled bear whirled around and charged toward the young brave. Ohgweluhndoe leaped to his feet and ran. Through the forest he went, dodging in and out among the trees, with Oh-gwa-li close behind.

Ohgweluhndoe knew he could not outrun the bear. Soon it would catch up to him and tear him

to pieces! Then there would be no one to take care of his young wife and baby son. He would have to fight for his life. So Ohgweluhndoe stopped running and turned to face the bear.

He lifted his arm to hurl his spear at the charging animal. Once again, luck was against him. The end of the spear caught in a twisted grapevine that hung from a young ash tree. This slender sapling was a little taller than Ohgweluhndoe and about as thick as his wrist.

Ohgweluhndoe tried to pull the spear free, but the lower end of the vine was tangled in a root at the foot of the sapling. All he did was to bend the sapling backward in a curve. Letting go of the spear, he turned and ran for his life.

Before he had gone very far, he realized that there was no sound behind him. He did not hear the bear's heavy feet crunching on the dry leaves. Looking back, he saw the bear lying on the ground with the spear through its neck. What had happened?

Ohgweluhndoe went back and looked down at the dead bear. Somehow the spear had come loose from the vine—with such force that it had killed the bear.

The warrior pulled the spear from the bear's neck. Once again he put the end of the spear against the vine. Slowly, he pulled the spear back. The vine stretched, bending the sapling. Ohgweluhndoe let go

of the spear. The sapling sprang upright. As the vine straightened with a snap, it hurled the spear through the air. Ohgweluhndoe had invented the bow and arrow.

The Iroquois soon learned how to make smaller bows out of smaller saplings. For the bowstring, they used animal hide instead of grapevine. They also learned to make small spears, or arrows, with feathers at the end to help them fly straight. The bow and arrow became their most important weapon.

From 1609 to Today

The children looked at their teacher with interest. He had just told them he was an Indian—a Mohawk Indian!

He smiled at them. "Let me tell you something about my people. They played a big part in the history of the United States. Why, if it weren't for them, you might speak French instead of English!"

"It was in 1609 when Mohawk warriors met the first white people they had ever seen. One of these men was the French explorer Samuel de Champlain. He was with a group of our enemies, Huron and Algonquin Indians. The French had guns—weapons we had never seen or heard of before. Champlain shot three of our chiefs, killing them.

Joseph Brant was a Mohawk chief at the time of the Revolutionary War in America.

"Mainly because of this, the Mohawk and our Iroquois brothers became bitter enemies of the French. Many years later, when France and Britain were fighting to gain control of North America, we helped the British. Some people who study history think that if we had helped the French, the United States and Canada would have become part of France." He grinned. "That is why I said that but for us you might be speaking French!"

"Yes," he went on, "we Mohawk and the other tribes of the Iroquois League were a great and powerful people. Our League had laws that ruled all the tribes. Each tribe had a number of people called sachems (SAY chuhms). The sachems represented their people at meetings of the great council. There, new laws were made and problems were solved. The League governed so successfully that the founders of the United States copied some of its ideas!

"We raided places as far north as James Bay in Canada to as far south as what is now Georgia—a stretch of more than 1,000 miles (1,600 kilometers). We conquered many tribes and believed our League might someday rule the world.

"But when the American colonies went to war with Britain, our League split. Two tribes sided with the Americans. We Mohawk decided to help our old friends, the British. Our chief, Thayendanegea, whom the British called Joseph Brant, led war parties against the Americans.

"To stop the attacks, American soldiers invaded our land. They burned our towns and killed our people. Most of us fled north, into Canada, which was British territory.

"The Mohawk at a French mission known as St. Regis remained in the United States. The mission became the reservation we call Akwesasne. It overlaps the U.S.-Canadian border. Ironworkers from Akwesasne earned a reputation for fearlessness while building bridges over the St. Lawrence River. Some of them moved to Brooklyn to build New York City skyscrapers. In 1977, a group of Mohawk moved to a new reservation in northeastern New York. Almost 20 years later, another group settled in New York's Mohawk River valley, the home the Mohawk had left 200 years earlier. Today the Mohawk in Canada and New York number about 10,000—more than all the Mohawk in North America when Champlain arrived."

Oren Lyons

Oren Raymond Lyons, a Seneca born March 5, 1930, used his lacrosse skills to get into college. Now he advises world leaders!

• In 1967, Lyons was selected to be a faithkeeper, someone who works to keep his people's traditions alive.

• In 1990, he helped negotiate the end of a confrontation between Mohawks and armed Canadian authorities.

• His experiences and Onondaga beliefs led him to speak to the United Nations about environmental protection and Native People's rights.

The Cherokee

People of the Southeastern Mountains

When Columbus reached America, the Cherokee were a large, powerful nation of about 25,000 people. They lived in some 80 towns in what are now the states of Alabama, Georgia, North and South Carolina, Tennessee, Virginia, and West Virginia.

The Cherokee lived in a land of high mountains. Thick forests covered the land. Birds and other animals were everywhere. The Cherokee got much of their food by hunting and fishing, but they were also farmers. They grew three kinds of corn, as well as other food plants.

The Cherokee called themselves Ani-yun-wiya, meaning "Real People." Other tribes knew them as "People of the Cave Country." The name Cherokee may come from the Creek word *tciloki,* meaning "people of a different speech."

Tribes closest to the Cherokee included the Creek, Chickasaw, Yuchi, and Tuscarora. A little to the north were the lands of the Shawnee and the Powhatan (POW uh TAN *or* pow HAT uhn). The Cherokee were often at war with one or more of these other tribes.

North America

CHEROKEE

A Cherokee Festival

Tree Climber stood on the riverbank with his mother and father and all the other people of the town. His mother held his little sister, The Pretty One, in her arms.

Tree Climber's father, Looks-to-the-Moon, gave the boy a little nudge. Taking a deep breath, Tree Climber walked with his parents down the bank and into the water. He waded out into the river until the water was nearly up to his chest. The water was bitterly cold, for it was early springtime, but Tree Climber gritted his teeth and did what he had to do.

Facing east toward the Sun, the Creator, Tree Climber ducked completely underwater seven times. His parents and everyone else did the same thing. The Pretty One cried a bit each time she was dipped into the water. Usually, dipping in cold water was a way to punish children who had been bad, but today, it was part of an important religious ceremony—the Festival of the First New Moon of Spring.

The ceremonies had started the night before, when the thin curve of the new spring moon appeared in the sky. The women started the festival of dances with the Friendship Dance. The dancing lasted until the moon set.

Just after dawn, everyone hurried to the meeting place in the center of the town. This building stood on a large, flat-topped mound. The mound had been built long ago. People had piled up thousands of basketfuls of earth into a great mound with slanting sides. Logs, placed lengthwise one above the other, formed stairs leading to the top.

The meeting place at the top of the mound had seven sides and a dome-shaped roof. A big building, it could hold all of the nearly 500 people of the town. Inside, three rows of benches, one above the other, ran around the walls. Seven stout posts, arranged in a wide circle, supported the roof. There was a second row of posts inside these, and a thick center post.

The seven sides of the meeting place stood for the seven clans, or family groups, of the tribe. The number seven was very important to Tree Climber's people. Tree Climber knew there were seven directions—north, south, east, west, above, below, and "here in the center." He also believed that there were seven heavens in the sky.

When everyone was inside the meeting place, the chief known as the White Chief, who was also the high priest, brought out the sacred crystal, which looked like a piece of glass. The people believed that the sacred crystal had the power to show the future. The priest stared into the crystal for a long time. Everyone waited silently. Finally, the priest announced that the corn crop would be good.

After that, everyone had gone to the river. Now, Tree Climber came out of the water, rubbing himself to warm up. His parents wrapped deerskin capes around their shoulders, as did many of the other grown-ups. Tree Climber's mother tucked The Pretty One under her cape.

Tree Climber was hungry. No one had eaten since yesterday, and there would be no food until

the great feast tonight. He decided to find some of his brothers and play war.

Tree Climber had a great many brothers and sisters—hundreds of them, in fact. For every child who belonged to his clan was counted as a brother or sister. Tree Climber and The Pretty One both belonged to the Bird clan. This was their mother's clan. Their father belonged to the Deer clan, the same clan *his* mother belonged to. When Tree Climber and The Pretty One grew up

The Cherokee

and married, they would marry someone from either the Wolf or the Long-Hair clan, the clans of their two grandfathers.

The town that Tree Climber and The Pretty One lived in was only one of many towns in the land of the Real People. Like all the other towns, it had two chiefs. The chief known as the Red Chief was in charge of war and games. He also represented the town when it was necessary to meet with other tribes. The White Chief was in charge of farming, religious ceremonies, the making of laws, and settling disputes.

The Red Chief was a young man. He had been chosen because of his many deeds of bravery and his skill as a warrior. The White Chief was an older man. He had been picked because he was well liked by everyone in the town. He was always good-natured, patient, and calm. The people called him "The Most Beloved Man."

Tree Climber liked and respected the White Chief, but he wanted to be the Red Chief some day! He often thought about being a brave warrior, like his father and like his mother's two brothers. War was very important to Tree Climber's people. The boy knew he could never truly be a man until he had fought bravely against his tribe's enemies.

This was why groups of young men often went forth to raid an enemy town. A woman known as the "Honored Woman," or "War Woman," often went with them. She did not fight, but she did tasks for the warriors and gave them advice. She also decided the fate of prisoners. She might decide that the prisoners should be adopted into the tribe, or she might decide they should be killed.

Tree Climber played war with some of his brothers for awhile. Later, he went into the woods with his mother to look for wild plant roots the family could eat. Time passed slowly for him. He was getting hungrier and hungrier!

Just before the sun set, everyone went back to the meeting place. A sacred fire always burned in its center. Now, the priest placed a deer's tongue in the flames. As the tongue burned, the people believed that the rising smoke carried their prayers to the Creator, the Sun.

After this, the people feasted. Then they danced in the big open square at the base of the mound. Everyone danced until it was nearly morning.

The holiday had been a joyous one. The people were thankful for the coming of spring. They were certain that the corn crop would be a good one this summer.

The Cherokee

Cherokee Ways

Cherokee women made flour from corn kernels as well as from sunflower seeds. They put the dried kernels or seeds into a hollow log. Then they crushed them by pounding them with a long, carved pole.

A Cherokee child usually had plenty of good food to eat. In summer, there might be a bubbling pot of corn and beans, together with broiled fish. In winter, there might be freshly baked, crunchy cornbread and smoked deer meat.

But in early spring, before the first crops were ripe, food was sometimes scarce. Then the Cherokee would eat just about anything they could find—such as bird's eggs, crayfish, turtles, and peanuts.

The Cherokee were good farmers. Each family had a large garden next to their house. In spring and summer, everyone worked to raise crops. They grew corn, beans, squash, and pumpkins, as well as sunflowers, grown for their tasty seeds.

Corn was the most important crop. The Cherokee grew three kinds. One kind was eaten roasted. Another kind was boiled with vegetables. The third kind was ground into flour and used to make cornbread.

There was plenty of wild plant food in the land of the Cherokee, too. Women and children gathered crab apples, persimmons, berries, grapes, cherries, mushrooms, and plant roots. In the autumn, they looked for walnuts, chestnuts, and hickory nuts.

Cherokee men often fished with a hook and line. They also speared fish and caught them in traps.

The Cherokee also had a way of catching a great many fish at one time. They mashed up the roots of certain plants. When they threw the mixture into the water, it "knocked out" all the nearby fish. The fish then floated to the surface and the men scooped them out of the water!

In late autumn and winter, Cherokee families, except for very old people, left their village from time to time. They would camp in the woods while the men hunted.

The Cherokee hunted mainly deer, which they shot with arrows. To hunt birds and small animals, hunters used a blowgun. This weapon, made from a hollowed-out reed, shot small darts when someone blew through it.

A Cherokee family had both a main house and a small house during cold weather. The family ate and slept in the main house most of the time.

The walls of the main house were made of poles stuck into the ground side by side to form a rectangle. Long, stiff reeds were then woven in and out, lengthwise, among the poles. This made a sort of screen that was then smeared with wet clay. The clay dried stiff and white, much like plaster.

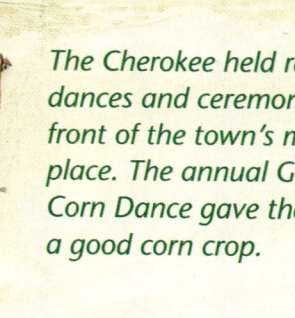

The Cherokee held religious dances and ceremonies in front of the town's meeting place. The annual Green Corn Dance gave thanks for a good corn crop.

A Cherokee family had two houses—a main house and a smaller winter house. Near their houses, each family had a garden in which they grew corn and other food plants.

The sloping roof was made of poles covered with reeds or tree bark. An opening in the roof let smoke out.

In the middle of the floor was a shallow pit for a cooking fire. A large, flat stone was always kept next to the fire pit. When the stone was heated on the fire, cornbread could be baked on it. The family stored food, tools, and other belongings against one wall. The beds, which were low platforms, were arranged against the other walls.

The family's other house was used for sleeping in winter or on cold nights. It was also used for taking sweat baths.

This house was small, low, and partly underground. The cone-shaped roof was made of poles covered with clay. There were beds and a fire pit in the cold-weather house. In cold weather, the fire was kept burning brightly all day. At night, it was allowed to almost go out. The little house would be warm as toast, but it was always smoky. The only way to let smoke out was to pull aside the skin that covered the entrance.

Most Cherokee clothing was made from deerskin. In the hot southern summers, a Cherokee man usually wore only a deerskin breechclout. Women wore a short skirt of deerskin. Everyone usually went barefoot.

In cold weather, or when hunting in the woods, men wore a shirt, leggings, and moccasins. The moccasins were like short boots. Women also wore such moccasins in winter. They also covered their shoulders with a short deerskin cape.

For special occasions, Cherokee men and women might wear a cape made of turkey feathers. Women made the capes by sewing feathers between narrow strips of bark. They then sewed all the strips together. Brightly colored feathers of other birds were sewn onto the capes as decoration. Not only was such a cape beautiful, it was also lighter than a skin cape and just as warm.

Cherokee Writing

For thousands of years, the Cherokee, like most other Indians of North and South America, had no way of writing. Then in 1809, a Cherokee man known as Sequoyah (sih KWOY uh) began inventing a way of writing the Cherokee language. He completed his project in 1821.

Sequoyah did this without knowing how to read or write English. He had no idea how letters were used to make words. He did not even know what an alphabet was, but he realized that every Cherokee word was made up of several different sounds. He found there were about 86 different sounds in the Cherokee language. So, he made up a symbol for each sound. By putting the right symbols together, he could write any Cherokee word.

For example, in Cherokee, Sequoyah's name, which means "sparrow," was made up of the four sounds *chee ss kwah yah*. So it is written with these four symbols:

ᏥᏍᏆᏯ

The artist who illustrated the Cherokee legend that starts on the next page is part Cherokee. His Cherokee name, Yah-nah-sah, means "buffalo." He signed his art with the Cherokee symbols for these three sounds.

bird	*chee ss KWAH*
butterfly	*kah MAH mah*
deer	*kah WEE*
I, or myself	*ah YAH*
people	*ah NEE*
wolf	*wah YAH*

In 1821, after 12 years of work, Sequoyah, a Cherokee man, invented a way of writing the Cherokee language. He did so without knowing how to read or write English. Here are some words as they are written with Sequoyah's symbols, and as they are spoken in Cherokee.

The First Fire

A Cherokee Legend

When the world was new, there was no fire. All the land was cold. The animals suffered terribly. The Thunders who lived in heaven took pity and sent a bolt of lightning to the earth. The lightning struck the bottom of a dead, hollow tree that stood on an island. The tree began to burn.

The animals saw smoke curling up out of the top of the tree, and knew fire was there. They held a council to decide how they might get some fire. Every animal that could fly or swim offered

to go to the island and bring back fire. Finally, the animals decided Raven should go. He was big and strong and should have no trouble.

Raven flew to the island and landed on the top of the tree. As he sat there trying to decide how to get the fire, a breeze sprang up. The flames rose and scorched all of Raven's feathers. This is why all ravens are black. Frightened by the heat and smoke, Raven flew back without fire.

Next to try was the little Screech Owl. He flew to the island and perched on the hollow tree. As he looked down into the fire, a blast of hot air shot up. The heat nearly blinded him. He managed to fly back to the council, but could not see well

after that. This is why a screech owl's eyes are red and why he blinks when he looks into light.

The animals of the council then decided to send two animals. The Hoot Owl and Horned Owl flew there together. By this time, the whole tree was burning fiercely. The smoke nearly blinded the two owls, and drifting ashes made white rings around their eyes. The owls had to come back without fire. No matter how hard they rubbed their eyes, they could not get rid of the white rings. This is why they still have white rings around their eyes.

The birds had had enough, but the little snake we call Black Racer said he would go. He was a good swimmer and had no trouble reaching the island. When he got there, he crawled through the grass to the tree.

The little snake crawled into a small hole at the bottom of the tree. There was so much smoke that he could not see anything, and the hot ashes burned him. He twisted and turned to escape the heat. Finally, he found the hole again. He crawled out, but he had been scorched black, as he is today. Ever since then, the black racer twists and turns quickly as he crawls, as if trying to get out of a tight, hot place.

Then, the big Blacksnake said he would try. He swam to the island and climbed up the outside of the tree. When he poked his head in at the top to see the fire, the smoke choked him—and he fell down inside the tree! Before he could climb out, he was scorched as black as Black Racer. This is why he is called Blacksnake.

After this, none of the birds or snakes or four-footed animals wanted to go near the burning tree. But unless one of the animals could get fire, the world would stay cold.

At last, Water Spider said she would go. Now, she can run across the top of the water and even dive to the bottom, so she had no trouble getting to the island. Then she had to stop and think. How was she to bring fire back?

She had an idea. She quickly spun some silk and wove it into a tiny bowl. Then she tied the bowl to her back. Creeping to the tree, she reached out with one of her long arms and scooped a tiny, glowing coal out of the fire. She put the coal into the basket on her back.

Then she ran quickly back across the water to the waiting animals. To this day, the big, black, red-striped water spider still carries a red bowl on her back. It is the one in which she brought fire to the world.

The Trail of Tears

The young man sat on a park bench. He was busily typing on a computer he held on his lap. A young woman came and sat down beside him. She watched him with curiosity. Finally, she asked, "Are you a writer?"

He stopped typing and nodded. "Yes. I am writing a book."

"What is it about?" she wanted to know.

"It is about my people, the Cherokee people," he told her. "I am a full-blooded Cherokee. My book is going to tell the story of a Cherokee family during the last 500 or so years."

"That sounds neat," she exclaimed. "Will you tell me a little about it?"

"Well," he said, "it begins when the Spanish explorer Hernando de Soto came into Cherokee territory. That was in 1540. He and his men were searching for gold, but when they found nothing, they left.

"About 100 years later, Frenchmen came, and then Englishmen. They were fur traders. They traded guns, metal tools, and other things with the Cherokee for the skins of animals. The Cherokee came to depend on the traders for almost everything. They no longer knew how to make stone tools and other things their ancestors had made. Their way of life had changed.

"By the 1700's, English settlers were coming into Cherokee territory to build homes and farms. The Cherokee had to give up some of their land to these new settlers. Then, in 1775, the American colonies went to war against Great Britain to make America a free nation. The British asked the

Cherokee to help them, and we did.

"When the Americans won the war, we ended up on the losing side. The American government made us give up a lot more land. We did the best we could on the land we had left. Most of the Cherokee turned to farming or business.

"Thanks to one man, a Cherokee named Sequoyah, nearly all the Cherokee could read and write in their own language. Sequoyah invented symbols for all the sounds in the Cherokee language, and so gave our people a way to write.

"By 1828, most of the Cherokee were well off. Some even owned big plantations and had slaves, just as many southern Americans did. We had formed a new nation, called the Cherokee Nation, and a government that was a lot like the government of the United States. We even had

In 1838, the United States government forced most Cherokee to leave their homes and move hundreds of miles west. About 4,000 Cherokee died during the long, hard journey, known as The Trail of Tears.

our own leader. He was John Ross, one of the greatest leaders the Cherokee ever had. We had our own schools and our own newspaper."

The young writer shook his head angrily. "They always talked about educating the Indians and making them just like white people, but we quickly found out that a lot of Americans really did not want that. What they wanted was our land!

"Even though the Cherokee land was protected by a treaty with the United States, it did not matter. In 1830, the government passed a law forcing all the Indians in the southeast to move west across the Mississippi River, into what is now Oklahoma.

"In 1838, the government sent 7,000 soldiers to round up the Cherokee and put them into camps. The local white people stole our animals and forced us out of our houses, but the worst was yet to come.

"In October, 1838, the soldiers began to force the Cherokee westward in groups of about 1,000. Most of the people were on foot. Winter struck while they were still traveling. They had to make their way through freezing rain, blizzards, and terrible cold. There was not enough food and there was no shelter.

"About 4,000 people—almost one-fourth of all those who started out— died of cold or disease! Often, the people were not even given time to bury their dead. To this day, we Cherokee still call that terrible journey the Trail of Tears.

"Not all the Cherokee left their home. About a thousand managed to escape and hide in the Great Smoky Mountains of North Carolina. They had a white trader, William H. Thomas, buy land for them with their money. This was a clever trick! The government could not take the land away because the deed was in the white man's name.

"The Eastern Band of Cherokee still lives in North Carolina. The reservation there is home to about 12,500 members. Surrounded by the scenic Smokies, many eastern Cherokee make their living from tourism.

"Another 16,000 Cherokee belong to the United Keetoowah Band, which has its headquarters in Oklahoma. The biggest group of Cherokee is the Cherokee Nation. It has 230,000 members. About 90,000 of these live on 7,000 square miles (18,100 square kilometers) in Oklahoma. This land is not a reservation. The Cherokee Nation, not the United States government, controls its development.

"With a multimillion-dollar budget and widespread lands, the Cherokee Nation seems more like a big business than a community. Yet its people have not forgotten their roots. In the words of Wilma Mankiller, the Nation's best-known chief in recent times, her people have succeeded because Cherokee culture 'has sustained us since time immemorial.'

"Mankiller's autobiography is basically a history of our people. We Cherokee have shown that we can come out on top in spite of all our troubles!"

The Osage

Village Dwellers of the Prairie

More than 300 years ago, about 6,000 Osage (OH sayj) lived mainly on the prairies at the southeastern edge of the Great Plains. This area takes in parts of what are now Arkansas, Kansas, Missouri, and Oklahoma.

The Osage believed they came from the stars. They named the sky, the earth, the waters, and all the animals. To themselves, they gave the name Ni-U-Ko'n-Ska, meaning "Children of the Middle Waters." The name Osage they got from Europeans. It comes from Wazhazhe, the name of one of the three bands that made up the tribe.

The Osage lived in villages near the edge of the plains. Two or three times each year, the Osage left their villages to go on a great buffalo hunt. The buffalo was their main source of food and clothing.

Each Osage village had two chiefs. One led the warriors in time of war. The other chief led all the people in time of peace. A group of wise men, known as "The Little Old Men," made all the laws and performed ceremonies.

Tribes living near the Osage included the Caddo, Illinois, Kansa, Kiowa, Missouri, and Quapaw.

North America

OSAGE

The Buffalo Hunt

The young boy known as Eats Grass squatted near the edge of the camp, listening for the distant thunder of hoofs. Very soon, he knew, the men would force the buffalo herd toward the cliff. Then he and everyone else would have plenty of work to do.

It was early summer, and hot on the plain. Eats Grass wore only a breechclout and moccasins. His head was shaved, so that only a fringe of hair ran around it. He could not wear the long hair-strip of a man. Eats Grass was only eight summers old—not even a person yet. He would become a person when he successfully completed his vision quest—the time when the Great Power would appear to him in a dream. Then, he would be given his name. "Eats Grass" was just a nickname his playmates had given him.

Nearly everyone from the village was on the buffalo hunt. Only a few old people, and women with very small children, had stayed behind. They would look after the crops that had just been planted.

The men, women, and children—and dogs pulling wooden frames loaded with supplies—had marched across the plain for several days. Along the way, they camped at places the tribe had used for generations. The two chiefs—the Sky People chief and the Earth People chief—had gone ahead to select a site for the hunting camp.

Eats Grass knew that the two chiefs took great care in choosing the place for the camp. It had to be near the cliff over which hunters would drive the buffalo. It also had to be a place they could defend. There was always a chance that while everyone in camp was busy after the hunt, their enemies, the Comanche and the Kiowa, might attack them!

Eats Grass found it exciting to come on this hunt with his father and mother. There had been work to do along the way, of course. Tender young plants were springing up on the plain, and many kinds were good eating. The people stopped often so the women and children could gather plants.

There had been time for play, too, especially in the evening at the camping places. Eats Grass and the other boys played buffalo hunt, with some of the dogs as buffaloes. At one camping place there was a stream with high, muddy banks. The boys played otter—sliding down the bank on their stomachs, into the water.

Suddenly, Eats Grass heard the great rumbling sound he had been listening for. He also heard loud shouts. The buffalo drive had begun!

He could imagine what was happening. His father, Reaches-the-Sky, had told him what went on. First, certain men went toward the herd. They kept the wind behind them, so the animals would smell them. This made the buffalo nervous. They began to move away from the smell. The men had picked a time when the herd was between them and the edge of a nearby cliff. To get away from the smell, the buffalo had to move toward the cliff.

Other men lay hidden behind piles of stone and brush on each side of the herd. As the buffalo began to move, these men jumped up, shouting and waving fur robes. The startled buffalo began to move faster to get away from the jumping, waving figures.

The buffalo were in a trap! The row of men on each side formed a big V. The buffalo were inside it. The point of the V was the edge of the cliff. The terrified buffalo had no choice. If they tried to go to one side or the other, the men quickly set fire to piles of brush. Frightened by the flames and smoke, the buffalo pressed close together. Staying between the rows of men, the herd stampeded toward the cliff.

When the animals at the front of the herd came to the edge of the cliff, they tried to stop, but it was not possible. The rushing animals behind them pushed them over the edge. Before the herd could stop, many buffalo had fallen off the cliff—breaking their legs and injuring

themselves so they could not move.

Other men, who had been waiting at the base of the cliff, went to work. They killed the injured animals with spears and clubs. Soon, great, shaggy bodies lay everywhere.

Then the work of skinning and butchering began. Every part of a buffalo was used for something. The skins were made into robes and other clothing. Hoofs were boiled down and made into glue. Horns were carved into spoons. The long, stringy tendons that connected muscles to bone were made into bowstrings. Hearts and stomachs were dried and used as bags. Fat was used for making paint. Bones became tools.

Most important, of course, was the rich, red meat. Men cut the meat off in strips. Eats Grass, with all the other children, the women, and old men, began to carry loads of meat back to the camp. There, the women dried the meat slowly in the sun, to preserve it. The whole village would live off the dried meat for several months.

The hunt had been a great success. Everyone was excited and happy. It was much like a holiday! While the women laid out the meat to dry, long lines of children continued to bring in more. Nearby, the men cooked the ribs of slain buffalo. That night, they would have a great feast.

Everyone had helped in the hunt, so the dead buffaloes belonged to all. The meat, skins, horns, tendons, and other useful parts were divided up among the clans, or family groups, of the tribe. There were more than 20 of these groups, with many people in each. The members of each clan would share the meat and other things among themselves.

These people, who called themselves the Children of the Middle Waters (and are now called the Osage), began to return to their village in late July. They stayed there while the women harvested the crops on their little patches of farmland. Then, in September, they set out again on another buffalo hunt. This hunt would provide them with a supply of meat for the winter.

Although the Osage hunted all kinds of animals, and raised corn and other crops, the buffalo was their main source of food and materials. The buffalo was very important to them. They thought of the buffalo as a sacred creature. They offered certain parts of the buffalo to the gods, who would in turn give them corn and squash and all the other things they needed.

Osage Ways

An Osage house looked like a wide, long hall with a low, curved ceiling. The walls were made of two rows of poles stuck upright in the ground. The tops were bent in and tied together. Other poles were tied crosswise. The Osage covered this framework with animal hides or mats made of dried plant leaves woven together. The mats overlapped so that wind and rain couldn't get in.

A row of stout posts down the middle of the house held up the roof. The house had two fireplaces, one on each end. The fireplaces were just shallow pits dug in the earth floor. The women who lived in the house did all their cooking in these fire pits. An opening in the roof above each pit let smoke out.

Most of the floor and walls were covered with woven mats like the ones on the roof. During the day, the Osage sat on the mats. At night, they slept on them.

Hanging from the walls and ceiling were skin bags of dried meat, ears of dried corn, braided lily roots, and strips of dried pumpkin. These were for wintertime meals. They had to be kept up high so the village dogs couldn't steal them.

Summers are long and hot in the prairie country where the Osage lived. Men usually wore only a deerskin breechclout and moccasins. Women wore a long skirt and a blouse or short cape around their shoulders. In very hot weather, they might wear only a skirt.

In cool weather, or when they had to walk through thick underbrush, men wore leggings for protection. The leggings had fringe that looked something like the feathers on the legs of a

farmland

main street

chiefs' houses

men's
bathing
place

women's
bathing
place

water lily
gathering
place

golden eagle. The Osage had a special liking for the golden eagle.

In cold weather, Osage men and women wrapped themselves in long robes of buffalo skin. The furry part was worn on the outside. The inside was often painted with designs and decorated with colored porcupine quills. The women made and decorated most of the clothes.

Osage women did all the farming on little patches of land near their village. In late summer, the women picked the corn. Some of it was boiled and eaten right away, but many ears were hung up to dry. Women ground the dried kernels into powder. The men often took plain corn powder with them to eat while away hunting. It was so light they could carry a lot of it. It did not taste very good, but it filled their stomachs. The powder was also mixed with water to make a kind of cereal.

The women also grew squashes and pumpkins. When these were ripe, the women peeled them and took out the seeds. Then they cut the yellow and orange insides into strips and hung the strips in the sun to dry. When the strips dried, the women braided them together and hung them in the houses for winter food.

The Osage were divided into two groups—Sky People and Earth People. The Sky People lived on the north side of the main street and the Earth People on the south side. All doorways faced east. The chief of the Sky People and the chief of the Earth People lived across from each other, in large houses. The chiefs usually had equal power, but the Sky chief led in time of peace and the Earth chief in time of war.

Osage warriors shaved off all their hair except for a narrow strip called a roach. They often tied animal hair and other decorations into the roach.

Women and children gathered many wild plants for food. A favorite was water lilies. The roots were boiled and the seeds were eaten raw or roasted, or ground into a flour. Persimmons (a wild fruit) were squashed into lumpy cakes. These cakes were baked over hot coals, on a flat wooden "frying pan." The Osage put their food in wooden bowls. They ate with spoons made from buffalo horns.

Women and girls wore their hair in braids. They painted the part in their hair red.

Quill Designs

You Will Need

- a cardboard box top
- scissors
- transparent tape
- drinking straws
- colored markers or crayons (optional)

The Osage, and other tribes of the Great Plains, used porcupine quills for decoration. They pressed the quills flat, dyed them different colors, and wove them through bark and leather. You can make quill designs with plastic straws.

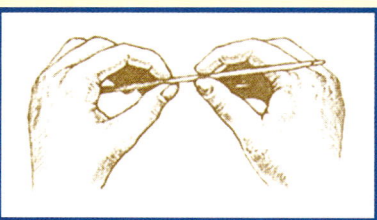

1 Flatten each straw by running your fingernail along it, hard, several times. Color the straws if you like.

2 With the scissors, make rows of slits in the box top, as shown. You may have to punch the holes with a sharp pencil first. Each slit should be a little wider than a flat straw. Leave a small space between slits.

top

3 Push a straw through an end slit, so only a small part sticks out on the underside of the box top. Fold this piece over and tape it to the underside. Push the rest of the straw through the end slit in the opposite row. Lace the straw through the other slits, back and forth from row to row.

underside

4 When only a short bit of the straw is left, tape it to the underside of the box top, as shown. Lace straws through the slits in the other rows in the same way.

The Land of My Fathers

The rancher patted the neck of his beautiful horse. "I really love horses," he said. "Maybe it's because horses meant so much to my ancestors."

"What do you mean?" asked his friend.

"Well, you know I'm three-quarters Osage," said the rancher, "and horses were mighty important to the Osage. For hundreds of years, they did all their traveling and hunting on foot. Then about 300 years ago, they got horses.

"An Osage legend tells that they got the horses from the Kiowa people, who lived farther south. After they got horses, the Osage soon became good riders. From then on, they hunted the buffalo on horseback.

"At about the time they got horses, the Osage also met the first European people they had ever seen. Two French explorers came to an Osage village. To the Osage, the men seemed pale and very hairy. The Osage called these foreign men I'n-Shta-Heh, or 'Heavy Eyebrows.' This became the Osage name for all white people.

"Later, more Frenchmen came to the prairie lands. They claimed it for France. They named it Louisiana, after the French King Louis XIV. Most of the French were traders. They gave the Osage metal axes, knives, and other things in exchange for furs. The Osage became very friendly with the French. When France was at war with Britain in the 1750's, Osage warriors helped the French.

"France lost the war, and Britain took over a large part of North America. This did not matter to the Osage. They lived far to the west of the British colonies, and it didn't matter after the colonies revolted and became a new country—the United States. At first, all this was too far away to make any difference to the Osage.

"But it soon began to matter. The United States started to grow. Americans began to move

westward, seeking open land for homes and farms. They pushed many Indian tribes off their old lands. Some of these tribes came into the land of the Osage. My ancestors often fought these invaders.

After the Osage got horses, they hunted buffalo on horseback. This painting by George Catlin shows an Osage on horseback lancing a buffalo.

"Then, in 1803, the president of the United States, Thomas Jefferson, bought the Louisiana Territory from France. The land of the Osage now belonged to the United States. Many Americans began to come here.

"To the Osage, these people were worse than the Indian invaders. They spoiled the land and drove the animals away. The settlers and the Osage were constantly fighting.

"The United States government offered the Osage gifts and rewards for giving up part of their land. They were to live at peace with the settlers and other Indians. The Osage feared they had to agree or the United States would send soldiers against them. In 1808, they signed a treaty. They gave up what is now most of the state of Missouri and part of Arkansas.

"Over time, the Osage surrendered more and more of their land. In 1872, the Osage moved to a big reservation in Oklahoma. American hunters had wiped out the herds of buffalo the Osage once hunted. So they now raised crops for food.

"In 1896, oil was discovered on the Osage reservation! Since then, the Osage have earned more than one billion dollars from oil and gas production."

The rancher looked across the grassy plain. "In 1907, the Osage reservation became Osage County—a section of Oklahoma with its own government, courts, and roads. Today there are about 18,000 Osage, but only about one-third still live in the county. They have farms and businesses and live much the same way as other folks in Oklahoma."

He paused again, and grinned. "We are living on the same land our ancestors lived and hunted on hundreds of years ago. That's more than most Americans can say!"

Maria Tallchief

A strict mother prepared Maria (Elizabeth Marie) Tallchief, left, an Osage born January 24, 1925, to become the first internationally known American ballet star.

• *Tallchief's mother enrolled her in ballet and piano lessons at age 3. Though skilled at both, she loved ballet.*

• *At age 19, Tallchief's talents captivated George Balanchine, a famous Russian-American choreographer from the New York City Ballet, who began creating roles just for her.*

• *Since retiring from the New York City Ballet, Tallchief has shared her expertise by teaching others.*

The Blackfeet

Wanderers of the Great Plains

The Blackfeet included three tribes—the Siksika (SIHK sih kuh), the Kainah (KY nuh), or Blood, and the Piegan (pay GAN). Each tribe had the same language and customs. In Canada, the Blackfeet are usually called Blackfoot.

About 200 years ago, there were some 15,000 Blackfeet. They lived in small bands in an area that stretched from what is now northern Montana in the United States to central Alberta in Canada. This is the northern part of the Great Plains. There, buffalo roamed by the millions. The Blackfeet lived mainly off the buffalo.

The chief of each Blackfeet band was chosen by the people of the band. He was picked because he was brave and wise. He did not make laws or give orders. The people simply followed his advice.

Other tribes that lived on the plains near the Blackfeet were the Cree, the Assiniboine, the Atsina (also known as the Gros Ventre), and the Crow. These tribes had much the same way of life as the Blackfeet. In the mountains to the west lived the Kutenai, the Flathead, and the Shoshone. The Blackfeet were often at war with one or another of their neighbors.

BLACKFEET

North America

The Winter Camp

The valley wore a coat of gleaming white snow. The river that snaked through the valley was silent and still, covered with thick gray ice. The trees clustered along the riverbank seemed like skinny, black skeletons without their thick summer thatch of leaves. The valley, like the rest of the vast plains country, was held tight in the cold, hard, silent grip of winter.

At one place beside the river there was noise and movement. In an open spot among the trees stood a dozen cone-shaped tepees. Blue smoke curled upward from the opening at the top of each tepee. A few figures moved among the tepees. Nearby, on the frozen river, a number of small figures raced about. This was a winter camp of a group of the people who called themselves Siksika, meaning the "Black-Footed People."

During spring, summer, and most of autumn, the Blackfeet followed the great herds of buffalo across the plains. But in winter, terrible storms lashed the plains. With snow piled as high as a tall man's chest, travel was impossible. So in winter, the camps of Black-Footed People stayed in one place.

They made a camp in a valley, beside a river and among trees. The valley gave them some protection from the fierce winds that swept the plains. The trees, acting like a snow fence, kept snow from piling up around the tepees. The trees also provided plenty of firewood. To get water, people chopped a hole in the ice on the river. On cold days, they huddled around the fires in their tepees.

Winter was a time for mending old things and making new ones. It was a time for telling stories or listening to them, but the people had work to do, too. They had to keep the fire burning in each tepee. Every day, the women went to gather armloads of tree branches. If a family's supply of smoked meat and dried vegetables and berries was running low, they also had to find more food.

A man stepped out of one of the tepees. He wore his buffalo robe, made of thick buffalo hide, with the fur inside. He carried a bow and arrows and a pair of snowshoes. He was going hunting with some of his companions.

They planned to make their way through the woods along the river. With luck they might find an elk or a few deer not too far away. They might have to search for several days, until they found some buffalo. In the summer, all the men of the camp hunted buffalo together, but in winter, the men hunted in smaller groups or in pairs.

If the men were lucky enough to find some buffalo, they would cover themselves with wolf skins. Then they would creep slowly toward the buffalo. The buffalo would pay no attention to the men because wolves could not harm the buffalo. When the men were close enough, they would kill one or more of the animals with their arrows.

As the man bent over to put on his snowshoes, he glanced toward the river. He looked to where the shouts and laughter of children resounded. His son and daughter were playing there with the other children of the camp.

The children played many different games on snow and ice. One favorite game was "hunting the buffalo." First, a group of girls slid down a snowy hill, each girl sitting on a large piece of buffalo hide. The girls played the part of the buffalo. The boys slid down after them, on sleds made of buffalo ribs. The boys played the hunters. When all the children were mixed up at the

The Blackfeet

bottom of the hill, each boy tried to poke a girl in the stomach and shout, "I got you now!"

Now the children played a sliding game on the icy river. A thin coat of snow made the ice good and slippery. The boys and girls ran and then let themselves slide. As they slid, they tried to see how many words they could shout before coming to a stop—or falling down.

The man smiled to see the children enjoying themselves. Then he started on his way. The snowshoes helped him to move quickly and easily over the snow.

In spite of the snow, the man saw early signs of spring. Before long the ice on the river would start to break up. The snow would begin to melt. Flocks of geese flying north would fill the air with their honking. Then it would be time to take down the tepees and move back to the open plains.

Blackfeet Ways

The most important and favorite food of the Blackfeet people was buffalo. They called it their "real food." They ate more buffalo meat than any other food.

The Blackfeet ate nearly every part of a buffalo—which could be used 52 different ways. Fresh meat was roasted or boiled. A soup was made from buffalo fat and blood mixed with wild berries. A kind of sausage was made by cleaning a piece of intestine, filling it with pieces of meat, and roasting it. Dried buffalo meat was pounded together with fat and chokecherries to make a hard, chewy food known as pemmican. Buffalo tongue, brains, and liver were all treats.

Before they had horses, the Blackfeet used dogs to help them carry things. A bundle was tied on a flat basket between two poles. The two poles were tied together at one end and fastened to a harness on the dog's back. A big dog could drag 75 pounds (34 kilograms).

The Blackfeet also hunted antelope, deer, mountain sheep, and small animals for food and skins. Most would not eat birds or fish, and, unlike some tribes, they looked upon their dogs as friends and would eat them only to keep from starving.

The Blackfeet did not grow any kind of food plant, but they did eat wild plants. The women and children used sharp sticks to dig up wild turnip roots and camass bulbs. They ate roots raw, roasted, or boiled. They also dried and stored them for winter. Then they used them in stews, with dried buffalo meat.

Berries and chokecherries were eaten raw or mixed into soups and stews. Many were dried to use in winter. When there were plenty of ripe, juicy berries, the Blackfeet often mashed them and drank the juice.

The Blackfeet usually ate two cooked meals a day, one in the morning and one in the evening.

In the days when they had no horses, Blackfeet men would wear the skin of a wolf to hunt buffalo. The buffalo were not afraid of wolves, so they paid no attention to the disguised hunters. The men could creep up close and kill a buffalo with arrows.

The Blackfeet

If they were moving camp, they might stop at noon to eat some dried buffalo meat, berries, or pemmican.

Like all Plains Indians, the Blackfeet were on the move most of the year. They had to keep following the buffalo herds. Each Blackfeet family had a cone-shaped tent called a tepee. *Tepee* comes from the Sioux word *tipi,* meaning "dwelling." This kind of house, which was used by all the Plains Indians, could be carried about and put up and taken down easily.

When a hunting group reached a camping place, the women put up the tepees. They held up the tepees with poles that they brought with them. The poles were the trunks of slim young trees with all the bark peeled off. The cover, made of a number of buffalo skins, was then wrapped around the poles and fastened in place.

Before the Plains Indians had horses, tepees were not very big. The size of the cover and the number of poles was limited by the weight dogs could drag or carry. After they got horses, the Indians made their tepees larger. The average smaller tepee was about 12 to 15 feet

To make a tepee cover, women sewed a number of buffalo skins together in a half circle. When finished, they had a feast to celebrate their work.

The Blackfeet

Blackfeet women always put up the family tepee. First, they tied the tops of four poles together. The bottoms of the poles were pushed into the ground to form a rectangle. From 12 to 20 more poles were leaned around the four poles to form a cone.

Next, the skin cover was stretched along another pole. This pole was lifted up and rested against the others. The cover was then pulled tight around all the poles and fastened in place.

Two other poles were pushed into the smoke flaps at the top of the tepee. The flaps were opened or closed by moving these poles.

Tepees were painted. Designs were animals or birds the tepee owner had seen in a dream. The top of the tepee was often painted black to stand for the sky at night. The bottom was painted red to stand for the earth.

Only Plains Indians wore feather bonnets, and only a chief or a great warrior could wear one.

When the Plains Indians got horses, their way of life changed. They could travel faster, carry heavier loads, and hunt more easily. War parties now rode horses when they went off to raid or to fight.

(about 3 1/2 to 4 1/2 meters) high and 15 feet (4 1/2 meters) across at the bottom. Two poles outside the tepee held the smoke flaps. By moving these poles, the smoke flaps could be adjusted to the wind, or closed if it rained or snowed.

The Blackfeet made their finest clothes from the skins of antelope or bighorn sheep. They usually made their everyday clothes of deer or elk

skins, or of cloth from the Europeans. During the hot summer days on the plains, the Blackfeet seldom wore much clothing.

In the winter, when it was often fiercely cold, a very important piece of clothing was a warm buffalo robe. It was made of one large piece of skin with the fur left on. The side without fur was usually decorated with designs that were painted or made of colored porcupine quills sewn in place.

Sign Language

The Indian tribes of the Plains did not all speak the same language, but these people often had to communicate with one another. So the Blackfeet and other tribes worked out a sign language to talk to each other.

Some of the signs used by the Plains Indians are shown below. In the picture to the left, the children are making the sign for "friend."

Father: *Touch the right side of your chest several times with your right fist.*

Mother: *Touch the left side of your chest several times with your right fist.*

I: *Point to your chest with your right thumb.*

You: *Point to person with your right thumb.*

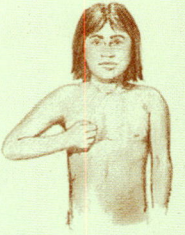

father   *I*

hungry   *dog*   *tepee*   *sleep*   *drink*

Thank you: *Hold your hands chest high, palms facing out. Push your hands slowly toward the person you wish to thank, letting your hands curve downward.*

Bird: *Hold your hands at your shoulders, as shown. Move your hands up and down, like the flapping of a bird's wings.*

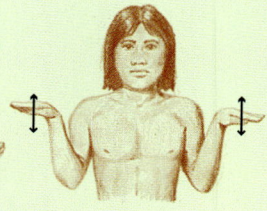

thank you   *bird*

The Proud People

The door slammed. A small, angry boy burst into the house. His mother saw he was upset. "What's the matter, Bill?" she asked.

"Aw, the guys were teasing me about being a Blackfeet," he said. "They told me if I washed my feet they would not be black anymore!"

His mother laughed. "I was teased like that, too. Don't let it bother you. Just tell them you are really a Siksika."

The boy looked puzzled. "I thought we were Blackfeet."

"We are. You see, *Siksika* means 'Black-Footed.' It probably refers to our moccasins, which were blackened by prairie fires, or dyed black.

"Some historians think that long ago, our people lived in the forest to the east, but they don't know why our people drifted westward. When they reached the plains, they split up into the Siksika, the Kainah, or Blood, and the Piegan. Today, all three groups are considered to be Blackfeet."

"Did the Blackfeet have horses when they were in the forest?" wondered the boy.

"No," said his mother. "Even after they reached the plains, the Blackfeet hunted and traveled on foot. There were not any horses in North America until the Spanish explorer Hernando Cortés brought them into Mexico in 1519. After a while, Indians got hold of some horses and learned to breed them. The Blackfeet got horses and guns about 1730. These changed their way of life.

"A trader from Canada came among the Blackfeet in 1754. He was the first white man the Blackfeet had ever seen. For a long time after that, the Indians and the white traders were friendly. But in 1806, when a group of Blackfeet met some Americans of the Lewis and Clark expedition, there was trouble. When the Blackfeet tried to steal some horses and guns from the Americans, the Americans killed two of them.

"The Blackfeet began to look upon all white Americans as their enemies. They named them 'Big Knives.' For many years, the Blackfeet fought to keep all American traders out of their country. At this time, our people also raided the Crow, Shoshone, Flathead, and other tribes to get horses. We were a warlike people.

Horses were wealth to the Indians of the Great Plains. So, the tribes often stole horses from one another. This painting by Charles M. Russell shows Blackfeet warriors on their way back from a horse-stealing raid.

"However, the United States government sent people to try to make friends with the Blackfeet, and in 1855, the Blackfeet signed a treaty. We agreed to let white people pass through our country, and even allowed a few to settle. Each year, the government gave us money, food, cloth, and other things.

The Blackfeet

"For a while, all was well. But as more and more white Americans settled on Blackfeet land, trouble started. Young Blackfeet warriors saw nothing wrong in going on horse-stealing raids against the white settlers, just as they did against other Indians. The raiders killed some white people and the whites killed some raiders.

"In January, 1870, a small force of United States soldiers attacked the winter camp of Chief Heavy Runner in Montana. They were after a few young braves who had killed a white man. It made no difference that this was a friendly Blackfeet band. The soldiers killed 173 men, women, and children and took 140 women and children prisoners. Most Americans were horrified by this dreadful massacre. The Blackfeet saw that they were helpless against the army. So the horse raids soon stopped.

"In the following years, government workers tried to get the Blackfeet to become farmers. They warned us that the great herds of buffalo might soon disappear. In time, this warning became very real. Thousands of white hunters killed the buffalo just for the skins. By 1890, the great herds had nearly disappeared. Where there had been many millions, only several hundred were left!

"This meant starvation for the Blackfeet and other Plains Indians. They had to depend upon the American and Canadian governments for food. Often, there was not enough, and many Indians starved to death.

"The Blackfeet way of life changed. We sold the land where we once hunted buffalo to the governments of the United States and Canada. We settled on reservations, became farmers and ranchers, and gave up our skin tepees for wooden houses.

"At first, things went well. Then in 1919, a dry summer destroyed most of the Blackfeet crop. A terribly fierce winter followed. Thousands of cattle and horses died. Many of the Blackfeet were left with nothing. Once again, we had to depend upon the government for food and help.

Elouise Cobell

One of nine children, Elouise Cobell, born on November 5, 1945, grew up on a Blackfeet reservation outside of Browning, Montana. She remembers her parents and grandparents wondering why they weren't getting paid regularly for letting the U.S. government use their land to farm and drill for oil.

Today, Cobell, an accountant and banker, is doing something about the problem. In 1996, she led a lawsuit with three other American Indians against the U.S. government for the mismanagement of Indian money and land throughout generations. It was one of the largest lawsuits ever brought against the federal government. Cobell continues her crusade as the case is worked out in the courts.

• In 1987, Cobell helped launch the Blackfeet National Bank in Browning, the first Indian-owned financial institution in the United States.

• In 1997, Cobell was awarded the "genius grant" from the MacArthur Foundation for her "exceptional merit and promise" in making a difference in society.

• In 2000, Cobell was declared a warrior of the Blackfeet Nation. She was presented with an eagle feather—the highest honor a Blackfeet can receive.

"With time, we recovered. About 20,000 of our people now live in the United States and Canada. Of those, about 4,500 Siksika, Kainah, and North Piegan live on reservations in Alberta, Canada. South Piegan, officially named the Blackfeet, farm and raise cattle on reservations in Montana. The rest live and work in towns. Although these groups have different leaders, they share the same culture and the Blackfeet language. It is one of the few Native American languages still spoken today."

She put her arm about her son and said, "Bill, the next time your friends kid you, remember, you are a Blackfeet—a Siksika—and we are a proud people!"

These Blackfeet chiefs take part in a powwow in Montana.

The Blackfeet 121

The Tlingit

People of the Northwest Coast

 The Tlingit (KLIHN kiht *or* TLIHNG giht) people lived along the coast of what is now southern Alaska and northern British Columbia, Canada.

Hundreds of years ago, many kinds of animals roamed the thick forests here, and immense numbers of fish and other creatures lived in the sea along the coast. Food was abundant in this region.

The Tlingit made and decorated many fine things. Their large houses in the winter villages were often painted and carved with decorations. Many of the men were skilled woodcarvers. Many women wove beautiful blankets.

Wealthy Tlingit men—and some women—gained status by giving a great feast called a potlatch (PAHT lach), at which they would give away much of their wealth. They would also gain wealth by going to potlatches given by other wealthy Tlingit. Some potlatches were held to mark births, marriages, and deaths.

Just south of the Tlingit lived the Haida (HY duh) and Tsimshian (TSIHM shee uhn) peoples. They were much like the Tlingit. To the north lived two very different groups of people—the Inuit and the Aleuts.

TLINGIT

North America

The Great Feast

The long, colorfully painted canoe, paddled by slaves, glided swiftly through the water. At the front of the canoe, a man in a bear costume danced about, tossing his head and waving his arms. At the back of the canoe, wrapped in fine blankets, sat a Tlingit leader, his wife, and their little boy.

The boy was excited. He and his parents were going to a great gift-giving feast to be held in honor of the raising of another leader's new memorial pole. This did not happen often, for it was tremendously expensive to give a feast of this kind.

Years might be spent preparing for such a feast. All of the relatives of the leader giving the feast had to help. Large amounts of food had to be stored up, because the feast lasted for days. Most important of all were the gifts—blankets, carved boxes full of fish oil, furs, and other things.

Then, at the feast, the leader would give all the gifts away! He might even destroy some, just to show how rich he was. A really great leader might give away almost all he owned. This proved his wealth and power. The more he gave away, the more honor and respect he gained. All of his relatives would share in his honor and respect, because they had helped him give the great feast.

The boy watched as the canoe headed toward a green strip of land in the distance. This was the island where the feast was to be held. Before long, the boy saw several tall, carved poles sticking up. Then the roofs of the houses came into view. The houses stood in a row on the beach. Behind the narrow beach, tall cedar and spruce trees covered the land.

A number of canoes from other villages were also heading toward the beach. Of course, everyone invited to the feast had taken great care to be on time. To be late was to insult the leader giving the feast.

The boy's father ordered his slaves to paddle the canoe to a place behind the others. He was a young man and had been a leader for only two years. All the men in the other canoes were older, more powerful leaders. It would not be proper for him to land before any of them. Such an insult might cause a war!

When the canoe finally landed, the boy's father, then his mother, and then the boy himself, stepped out, very slowly and solemnly. The slaves followed with the family belongings— bowls, spoons, baskets, finely carved boxes for holding fish oil, sleeping blankets, and other items.

A relative of the leader who was giving the feast greeted the boy's father. The family's bowls were filled with good things to eat. Slaves filled their beautifully carved boxes with tasty fish oil.

The boy's basket was filled with berry cakes, but he would find that this was only the beginning. He and his parents would receive many more things. They would have so much food they would not be able to eat it all.

Together, the family walked solemnly toward the feast-giver's house to meet him. The great leader and his wife stood beside the door. The

leader was wrapped in a beautiful blanket decorated with emblems of his family. On his head he wore a special headdress of ermine tails. He greeted the young leader graciously. The boy's father was very respectful in return. The great leader's wife greeted them with a special smile, for the young leader was one of her relatives.

When he entered the house, the boy could hardly believe his eyes. Never had he seen so much food and wealth! Huge boxes of fish oil and piles of blankets and fur robes lined the wall. The smell of smoked salmon, chunks of roasting deer and bear meat, and baskets of berries and tasty roots made his mouth water. There was even a copper—one of the big, flat pieces of decorated

copper worth
thousands of blankets!

For the rest of the day, the boy and his
parents spent their time meeting the other guests,
listening to singers, watching the dancers and
actors—and eating. The merriment went on long
into the night, with everyone grouped around the
blazing fire in the great leader's house. Once, the
boy almost shouted with delight when the leader
had a slave throw a whole box of costly fish oil
into the fire. The flames shot up almost to the
roof. How wealthy the leader must be to burn up
so much fish oil!

On the third day, the real business of the feast
took place. The guests sat on mats of woven cedar
bark outside the great leader's house. The

wealthiest and most powerful leaders sat closest to the leader giving the feast. Less important leaders sat farther away. Each man knew exactly where he belonged.

When all was ready, the Speaker stepped forward. He was a specially chosen man, a leader himself, as great as the leader giving the feast. He carried a carved wooden staff, the "talking stick," that showed he was the Speaker. Holding up his staff, the Speaker shouted, "The time has come to raise the memorial pole."

Until that moment, the pole had been hidden. Now, a crew of

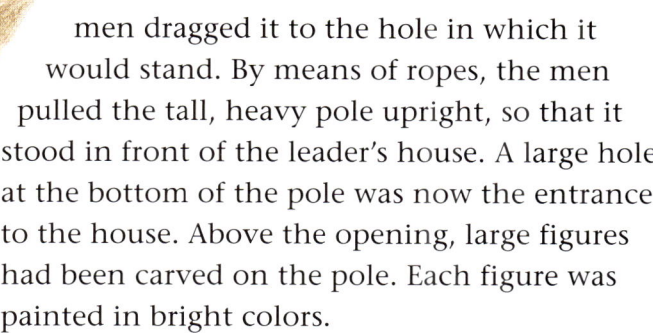

men dragged it to the hole in which it would stand. By means of ropes, the men pulled the tall, heavy pole upright, so that it stood in front of the leader's house. A large hole at the bottom of the pole was now the entrance to the house. Above the opening, large figures had been carved on the pole. Each figure was painted in bright colors.

The boy listened carefully as the Speaker told the stories of all the figures, and why each was important to the leader. The stories took a long time, but the boy enjoyed them. They explained why the leader was so important. Many of the great people in the leader's family had been helped by spirit animals. The figures on the pole stood for some of the people and animals.

The stories over, dancers came leaping and shouting to entertain the guests. They wore masks and special costumes. Their dances acted out the stories the Speaker had told.

Much more happened during the day. Children of the leader's family-group who had reached a certain age were introduced to the guests. Then there was more dancing—and more eating. Finally, the time came for the great gift-giving.

The leader started with the most important guest. He gave this man blankets, fur robes, and other valuable things. The boy knew by the way the man accepted the gifts that he was pleased. If the man had thought the presents were not good enough, he would have dragged the blankets on the ground as he walked away. This would have been a dreadful insult to the leader!

Each of the other guests, in order of importance, received similar presents. The boy was excited, for he could see that the leader had given away almost everything.

The leader then picked up the copper that was worth a fortune in blankets. To show that he had so much wealth it did not matter, he cut off a large piece from the copper and threw it into the fire, where it melted.

Truly, the great gift-giving feast had been wonderful. The leader had shown he was an important and wealthy man. The boy knew that the leader would get back all—and perhaps more than—he had given away. For every man who had been a guest would now have to hold a gift-giving feast.

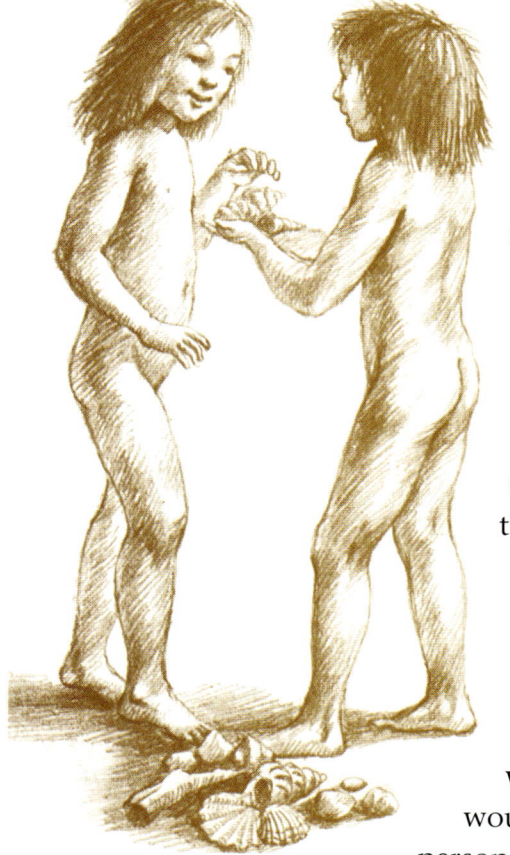

The leader would be invited to each feast. He would receive many fine gifts. The men holding the feasts would try to give the leader more presents than he had given them. Even though the leader had given away most of his wealth, he hoped to get back much more!

When the time came to leave, the boy eagerly climbed into his father's canoe. He was anxious to get home so that he could play at having a gift-giving feast. He and the other children would use sea shells, stones, and bits of wood for the gifts.

The boy knew that when he was older he would go to live with his mother's family. They would help him gain wealth. One day he would have many blankets and robes. Then he would hold a real gift-giving feast. He would show what a great and important person he was.

Tlingit Ways

A Tlingit never went hungry. There was plenty of food for all the people who lived along the northwest coast. From the ocean, they got many kinds of fish and sea animals such as seals, porpoises, and sea otters. Along the shore, plenty of clams could always be found. In the nearby mountains and forests, men hunted bears, deer, and mountain goats. Women gathered berries, wild plant roots, and seaweed.

One of the most important Tlingit foods was fish oil. This came from a small fish called a candlefish. The fish was boiled until the oil came out. The oil was skimmed off the water and stored in wooden boxes. The Tlingit used the oil to preserve many foods. They also dried the fish. Then they put a wick into its mouth and burned it like a candle!

The Tlingit ate one meal late in the morning and another at sunset. People usually ate in their houses. They sat on the wooden floor. The food was placed on a mat made of woven cedar bark. Before eating, people rinsed their mouth with water. This was good manners—and good manners were very important to the Tlingit, especially when they ate.

After they rinsed their mouth, people washed their hands and face in a bucket of water. Then they dried themselves with a napkin woven from soft, shredded cedar bark.

Each person then took a drink of water from a special drinking bucket. Everyone took a long drink. They would not drink again until the meal was over. To drink during a meal was very bad manners.

A meal might begin with dried fish, which they ate with their fingers. Next came the cooked food. This was served in wooden dishes. People ate this part of the meal with spoons carved from the horns of mountain goats. Everyone was careful to take only small sips and never open their mouth wide enough to show their teeth while they were eating. That would be very impolite. After finishing the cooked food, the people again washed their hands and face.

The final course might be a big bowl of dried berries mixed with fish oil. When the meal was over, everyone again washed their hands and face. Now that the meal was over, they could all take a long drink of water.

In summer, most Tlingit men worked in or near the sea. Because the weather was warm and they were often soaking wet, they wore only a deerskin breechclout. Women usually wore a skirt and shawl woven from cedar bark.

In winter, both men and women wore deerskin shirts and pants. In cold or rainy weather, men and women wrapped themselves in blankets woven from cedar bark. They might also wear woven hats made of spruce roots. These looked like upside-down baskets. On the coldest days, both men and women wore moccasins. They wore snowshoes to walk on the snow.

The Tlingit and their neighbors were the only Indians who built their houses out of wooden boards, or planks. A Tlingit village looked much like a group of big barns clustered together. The first white people to come to the Northwest were impressed to see these large wooden buildings

made with stone tools and put together without nails.

Tlingit houses were commonly made of wood from cedar trees. Men went into the forests for them. Then they cut down the trees, trimmed them—with only stone tools for the job—and brought back the logs. It took a lot of time and many people to build a Tlingit house. Only a wealthy and important man, such as a leader, or head of a household, owned a house.

The house was started by building a frame of stout logs and heavy beams. Then the sides and

A Tlingit village looked much like a group of big barns clustered together. Tlingit houses were often made of wood from cedar trees.

The Tlingit   133

roof were covered with planks. To make the planks, men pounded wedges into the ends of cedar logs. This caused long flat pieces to split off. The Tlingit knew how to split logs into boards almost exactly the same size.

When a house was finished it might be as much as 50 feet (15 meters) long and 40 feet (13 meters) wide. Several families lived in each house. The house had no windows. The doorway was a large round or oval hole.

The floor of the house was made of planks, too. There was usually a built-in bench running

Women wove the blankets that Tlingit people wore. As they worked, the women followed patterns painted on boards that they kept beside them.

all around the inside walls. In the middle of the floor was a large pit, used as an open fireplace. All the women of the house shared the fire to cook for their families. Boards in the roof above the fireplace could be slid aside to make an opening to let smoke out and some light in.

A Tlingit village usually had only a few of these big houses, built close together in a row. The villages were by the sea. The doorways of the houses always faced the water.

At the back of a Tlingit house were sleeping compartments for the leader and other important people. The compartments were often small copies of the main house. The leader's compartment was usually painted with designs.

Totem Poles

Raven

Eagle

Hawk

Beaver

Thunderbird

In the villages of the Tlingit—and most other Northwest Coast people—there were usually many tall poles. Carved on the poles were great grinning and frowning figures, one above the other.

These poles are now called totem poles. A *totem* (TOH tuhm) is a symbol, usually an animal, that stands for a tribe, clan, family, or person. A totem pole was a sort of "signboard" that told about a person's family. Some totem poles served as entrances to houses, while other totem poles stood alone. Only leaders or wealthy heads of households could afford to have totem poles. The poles announced the greatness of family, honored a family member who had died, or marked an important family event.

Some of the figures on a totem pole stand for ancestors. These are often shown as animals, because the Tlingit believed that magic animals started their families. They also believed that magic animals had often helped or even married some of their ancestors. All this was told in family legends. The person who bought the pole picked out the parts of the legend he wanted to show on the pole.

The artists who carved totem poles were greatly respected and well paid. They carved the magic animals the same way on every pole. Raven always had a straight beak. Eagle had a curved beak. Hawk had a beak that curved nearly all the way back. Beaver had two big front teeth. The mythical Thunderbird— who made thunder by flapping its wings and lightning by blinking its eyes—had outstretched wings.

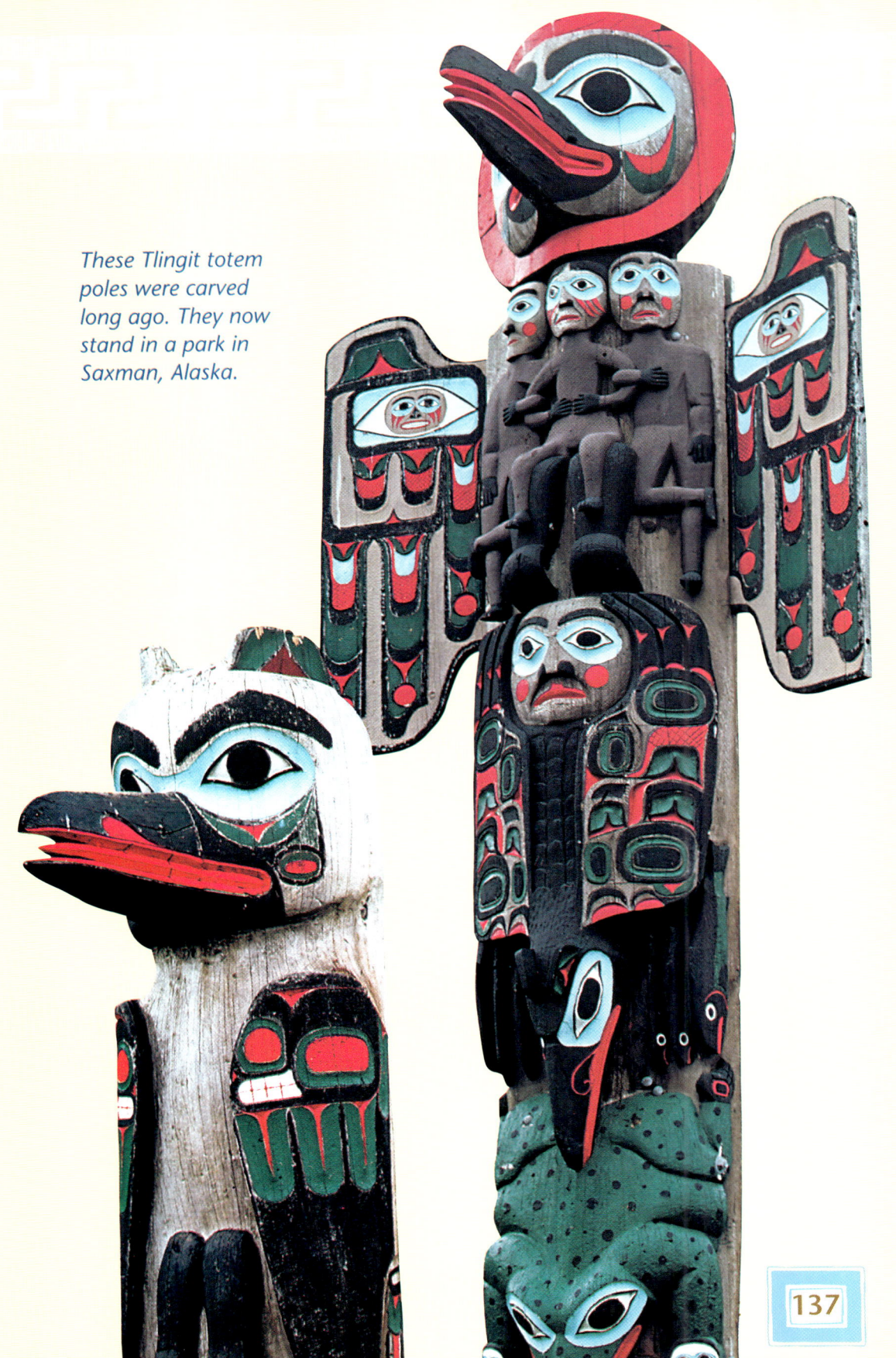

These Tlingit totem poles were carved long ago. They now stand in a park in Saxman, Alaska.

Furs, Gold— and Poverty

The captain of the fishing boat wore a red checkered shirt and blue jeans. He looked like all the men who made a living fishing off the coast of Alaska, but there was one difference. The captain was a Tlingit.

He stared at the distant, snow-tipped mountains. "Things are better now for some of us," he said, "but many of us are still poor." He shook his head sadly. "Long ago, we had plenty. That was before the Russians came here in a ship in 1741. They were the first white people we met. It was not a friendly meeting. Some Russians came ashore in two boats, to get fresh water. Our people killed them and took both of the boats!

"When the men did not come back, the ship sailed away. The Russians claimed the land. They named it Alaska, from an Aleut word that means 'great land.'

"In 1799, the Russians came back. They built a fort near where the city of Sitka is now. In 1802, the Tlingit attacked the fort and killed most of the settlers. Two years later, the Russians attacked and beat us badly. For many years after that, our relations with the Russians were tense.

"In 1867, the United States bought Alaska from Russia. We resented these settlers, too, and often fought for our land.

"In 1896, whites discovered gold in a place north of here called the Klondike. Thousands of people came, hoping to become rich. Suddenly, everything changed. Many gold hunters took our land. Soon, all we had left were our villages. To survive, Tlingit men took factory jobs, packing fish in cans.

"For years, the Alaskan tribes asked the United States government to pay for the land that was taken from us. Finally, in 1971, the government returned to the Alaskan

The Tlingit

Tlingit and Tsimshian dancers perform at a potlatch in Metlakatla, an island in Alaska. The potlatch was held to honor a man who had lived and died on the island.

Indians 44 million acres (18 million hectares) of land and millions of dollars as payment. The Tlingit and other Alaskan Indians called the Haida have formed the Sealaska Corporation, to make the most of the money and land.

"But the Tlingit must constantly guard their land and rights. In the 1990's, they struggled to protect the rights of all Alaskan Indians, those living in cities as well as in the country, to hunt and fish on public lands.

"Some of our greatest treasures are the traditions we keep alive. We have rebuilt old houses to use for potlatches and funeral rites. Many Tlingit are learning to carve totems and weave blankets, just as their great-grandparents did."

The Pomo

People of California

The Pomo people lived on the west coast of North America, just north of what is now San Francisco Bay, California. A few hundred years ago, there were between 10,000 and 20,000 Pomo. Some lived along the seacoast, others by rivers or lakes, farther inland.

The climate in this land is mild all year long. Near the coast lie forests of giant redwood trees. Farther inland are grassy valleys and forests of oak.

The Pomo always had plenty of food. They hunted the birds and animals of the forest. They fished in the Pacific Ocean and in lakes and rivers. They gathered acorns, berries, and other wild plant food.

The Pomo had many small villages. Each village had a headman who saw that religious ceremonies were held and that children were taught the proper way of life. He also entertained visitors and kept peace among the villagers.

Tribes living near the Pomo were the Maidu (MY doo), Miwok (MEE wahk), Patwin (PAT wihn), Wappo (WAH poo), and Yuki (YOO kee). All these people lived much like the Pomo.

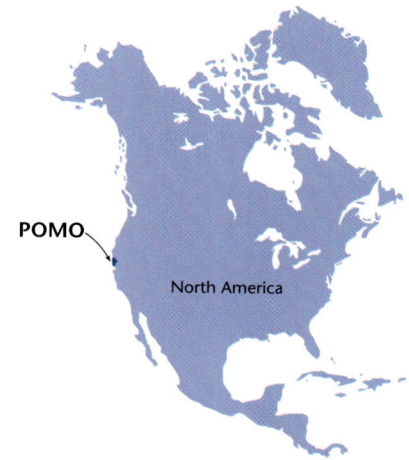

POMO

North America

The Ash Ghosts

The little girl was frightened. She sat huddled as close as she could to her mother. They were alone in the dark house, and soon, the Ash Ghosts would come!

Most of the time, life in the village was uneventful. All the days were much alike. The girl's father hunted or fished, or he might stay at home to make a weapon or a tool that was needed. The girl's mother spent a great deal of time gathering wild plants to eat, or she might spend the day weaving a basket. At night, families visited with each other. Then, the old people told stories of Coyote, the Creator.

But today had been different. It was the time of the Ghost Ceremony, when both the ordinary ghosts and the Ash Ghosts would dance through the village. The ordinary ghosts wore many feathers on their heads. Their bodies were covered with paint. They danced during the day.

The Ash Ghosts danced at night. They wore only a few feathers on their heads and a veil of leaves to cover their faces. They, too, had painted their bodies from head to foot. In their hands they carried their badge of office—a crooked stick, with one end carved to look like the head of a bird. A few of them also carried live rattlesnakes!

Now, it was after sunset. The village lay in darkness. The girl knew that all the women, girls, and small boys were hiding in their houses. All the men and older boys were at the big dance house. No women and children would be allowed there tonight.

A deep, booming *buroom-buroom-buroom* came from the dance house. Two men were stamping on the foot drum—a hollow log placed over a shallow pit.

Suddenly the booming stopped. For a time, the village was silent. Then came another sound—a loud, long whistling moan!

"What is that?" squeaked the girl.

"The voice of the dead," whispered her mother.

The girl stiffened in fear and clutched at her mother's bark apron. She could hear sounds outside the house! She could see flickers of light. The Ash Ghosts!

The men playing the parts of the Ash Ghosts moved quickly through the village. Some of them carried torches. Those who had rattlesnakes peered into some of the houses, shaking their rattlesnakes at the frightened women and children. Then all of the men and older boys entered the dance house.

In the dance house, the older boys were being initiated into the secret society to which all the men belonged. The initiation ceremony lasted four days.

Throughout the ceremony, the Ash Ghosts acted like both clowns and magicians. They danced about a fire. Sometimes they even stuck their heads into the flames and ate the burning coals.

At one point in the ceremony, the Ash Ghosts grabbed the boys, picked them up, and tossed them back and forth through the flames of the fire to frighten them. The Ash Ghosts then spoke seriously to the boys. They told them that pain and fear are a part of life.

Toward the end of the ceremony, the headman of the village spoke. He told about the laws of life and the way young people should live. The best kind of person, he told the boys, is a hard worker who is kind to everyone and does things to help the whole village. Each boy, he said, should try to be this kind of person.

Now the boys had become men. They joined in a big feast that ended the ceremony.

After the ceremony, life in the village went on as it had before. The people went about the important business of finding food. The Ash Ghosts were gone. They would return when the next great ceremony took place.

The Pomo

Pomo Ways

In northern California, where the Pomo lived, the climate is usually mild all year. So the Pomo people did not wear much clothing.

Pomo women usually wore two aprons. One was narrow and worn in front. The other was larger and worn in back. Women who lived near a lake or river usually made their aprons out of rushes that grew along the shore. In villages near the redwood forests, aprons were generally made of redwood bark. Sometimes, though, the women wore a deerskin skirt.

Most of the time, Pomo men wore nothing at all. When they did, it was just a deerskin breechclout. But on chilly nights or cool, rainy days, men and women wrapped themselves in warm, thick robes made of strips of rabbit skin woven together.

Pomo men and women did, however, dress up for special occasions. Their dress clothes were very colorful. They had headbands made from the orange and black feathers of the flicker. Women wore necklaces made of shell, stone, and bone beads. Both men and women had their ears pierced. In the holes in the ear lobes they put long wood or bone rods with tufts of bright feathers at each end. The men also painted their faces and the bare parts of their bodies black, blue, or white.

The Pomo lived in villages that varied in size from about 50 to 300 or more people. There was no wall around a Pomo village, and there were no streets. The houses were built wherever people felt like putting them.

Pomo men usually spent most of their spare time in a sweat house. This place was like a club for them. They talked, played games, and even slept there.

The kind of houses the Pomo built depended upon where a village was located. Near a redwood forest, the houses were made of redwood bark. They were very simple houses. First, a pole that was forked at the top was stuck in the ground. Then, long pieces of bark were leaned on a slant all around the pole. Only one family of four or five people lived in such a house.

The Pomo who lived near a lake or river made larger, dome-shaped houses. First, they stuck a

number of thin poles into the ground to form a circle. They bent the tops of the poles in toward each other and tied them together. This framework was then covered with bundles of dried grass or dried rushes. Two or three families lived in such a house.

In every Pomo village there was a dance house. This was a large circular building, as much as 60 feet (12 meters) across. It was simply a round pit dug in the ground and covered over with a dome-shaped roof of earth and dried grass. It was used for special religious ceremonies.

Every Pomo village had at least one sweat house. This was just like the dance house, only smaller. Men and boys usually took a sweat bath every day, sitting in hot steam to purify their bodies.

One of the most important Pomo foods was acorns. Acorns are the nuts of oak trees. We do not eat them because they are bitter, but the Pomo knew how to take out the bitterness.

In autumn, when oak trees are filled with acorns, each Pomo village held a great harvest. Men and boys climbed the trees to shake down the acorns. The women and girls gathered them

After shelling acorns, the Pomo women used stones to grind the nuts into powder. The powder was then spread out in watertight baskets. Next, they poured hot water over the powder. This took out the bitterness and left a sticky dough.

and put them into baskets. Enormous amounts of acorns were gathered and stored away.

The Pomo also ate many other kinds of plant food. They gathered berries and the roots of wild vegetables. They were fond of the young, tender leaves and stems of many plants. They also ate seeds and flowers.

There were deer, rabbits, and many kinds of birds in Pomo country. Men caught birds and small animals in traps. They shot larger animals with arrows. Meat was broiled over a low fire. Some was cut in strips and dried in the sun. Then it was stored until needed.

There were also fish in the rivers, lakes, and ocean. Men usually used nets to catch fish. Fish, too, was either broiled or dried and stored.

Pomo people often ate such things as boiled and roasted caterpillars, grasshoppers, and other insects. These may not sound very good to you, but if you had been a Pomo child, you would have enjoyed them!

Acorn dough was mixed with water to make a paste. The paste was then put into a basket. The women cooked the paste by dropping hot stones, heated in a fire, into the basket. The result was a tasteless pudding.

Pomo women wove some of the most beautiful baskets in the world. They used the baskets to cook and to hold things.

The Troubles of Coyote

A Pomo Legend

There was a time when the world had no creatures living on it. So Coyote made some people out of rocks. He put the people into valleys to live. Then Coyote made all the different kinds of animals. He put them onto mountains to live. He put all the birds on one mountain. He sent all the furry creatures to another mountain. The lizards went onto a third mountain, and he put all the snakes onto a fourth mountain.

Coyote was pleased with most of the creatures he had made, but as he watched the people, he became angry. He had wanted people to live in peace. He had meant them to spend their time catching fish and gathering seeds to eat. Instead, they were often at war and doing bad things to each other. So Coyote sent a great flood into the valleys. All the people drowned.

Now the valleys were empty. Coyote made new people and put them into the valleys to live, but these people were no better than the first ones. Again Coyote became angry. He sent a raging fire to kill all the second people.

The fire also burned the mountains. Most of the lizards and snakes were roasted. Coyote was hungry. So he ate the lizards and snakes.

After eating, Coyote was very thirsty. He searched for days until he found water. He drank so much water that he swelled up. For four days

he was dreadfully sick. Finally, Bullfrog came to his aid. With a stone knife, Bullfrog cut a hole in Coyote. All the water ran out of Coyote and formed a great lake.

Now Coyote made some more people, but these people were bad, too. The angry Coyote sent a whirlwind to kill them. The whirlwind also blew among the mountains. It blew the animals living on the mountains into all parts of the world. This is why you now find all kinds of animals everywhere.

Then Coyote made a fourth kind of people, but these people were just as bad as the others. So Coyote sent ice and snow to freeze them to death.

Finally, Coyote made a fifth kind of people. Most of them went to live near the big lake that had been made when Bullfrog opened up Coyote to let the water out. They stayed at peace. They lived the way Coyote wanted them to. They were The People—The Pomo.

Gold and Destruction

The art teacher was showing her students how to weave a basket.

"There," she said as she finished. "Not bad, but my great-great-grandmother would have done better. She was a Pomo, and Pomo women made the most beautiful baskets in the world. No one knows how to make baskets quite like them anymore."

"Why not?" asked a student.

"Because the Pomo have forgotten many of their old ways," said the teacher, sadly. "Pomo people have probably lived in California for as long as 1,500 years. During most of that time, their way of life hardly changed at all. Then, about 200 years ago, things began to change."

"What happened?" another student asked.

"We met white people for the first time. They were Russians. They came here in 1812. A few years later, the Spanish, and then the Mexicans came. A mission was built at Sonoma. Cattle ranchers came into part of our land. Then, in 1848, California became part of the United States.

"That same year, gold was discovered in California. Thousands of people rushed to the gold fields. Before long, settlers moved in here. They cut down the oak trees and killed off the animals to make homes and towns for themselves. Without acorns and game, many of my people starved. Others died of diseases brought by the settlers.

"The white people looked upon the Pomo as savages. They even hunted the remaining Pomo, like animals. The peaceful Pomo did not try to fight. Many of them worked for the settlers instead. The settlers were glad to hire them, because they asked for little in wages.

These Pomo dancers perform in traditional dress at a Big Time gathering as part of the Marin County Museum's Trade Feast in Novato, California. This large social gathering also features Native American food, arts, demonstrations, and crafts.

"The Pomo ended up on reservations, called *rancherias*, in California. These covered only a fraction of our ancestors' land. In the 1950's, the U.S. government offered to build roads and bring water and electricity to the rancherias. In return, it wanted the right to sell or use Pomo land. The Pomo agreed, but the government never made any improvements. My people received nothing and now lived on land they did not own.

"In the early 1980's, Pomo Tilly Hardwick sued the government for the people on 17 rancherias. As a result, the people recovered some of their land. Today Pomo live on 19 California rancherias with populations of 15 to 500.

"Before the settlers came, there were between 10,000 and 20,000 Pomo. Today, there are less than 5,000. Almost one-third of them live on Pomo lands."

The art teacher sighed. "I don't know everything about my ancestors' ways, but I do know I can't make baskets as beautiful as Pomo women used to make!" She held up her slightly awkward basket.

The Hopi

Village Dwellers of the Southwest

The Hopi (HOH pee) lived in the Southwest United States, in what is now Arizona. This is high desert country. Large, flat-topped, steep hills, called mesas, dot the broad land. Mesquite, cactus, and other desert plants grow here.

Several hundred years ago, at least 7,000 Hopi lived in villages on top of some mesas. They built stone houses covered with clay. These houses, all joined together, made a Hopi village look like a large apartment complex.

Very little rain falls in this country. When it does rain, the water runs down the sides of the mesas and soaks into the ground below. The Hopi had farms on the land below the mesas on which their villages stood. Most of their food came from their farms.

The Hopi did not have a central tribal government. Families in each village had their own leader who cooperated to settle disputes.

Living close to the Hopi, and much like them, were the Zuni (ZOON yee) and Keresan (KEHR uh suhn) peoples. Nearby were the Havasupai (hah vuh SOO peye) and Walapai (WAHL uh peye), who lived in the canyons of the Colorado River. The warlike Navajo and Apache also lived in this desert area.

North America

HOPI

Life in the Desert

Bird-Ready-to-Fly sat on the ground beside her grandmother, Flute Woman. They were making baskets of dried, twisted plant leaves. Flute Woman's basket would be perfect, for she had made baskets for many years. She was an old, wise, and skillful person, but Bird-Ready-to-Fly was only 8. She was just learning how to weave a basket. She was not very good at it yet. Already, her basket looked lopsided!

The leaves for the baskets came from plants that grew in the desert. The desert was the home of Bird-Ready-to-Fly's people, the Hopi, which means "Peaceful Ones." It was a harsh, dry land, but the Hopi knew how to get everything they needed from it.

Just the other day, Bird-Ready-to-Fly had watched some of the women build a new house. They built the walls with stones the men brought from the desert. Then they coated the stones with moist clay dug out of the desert. The clay dried smooth and hard in the warm sun.

Women also made pottery out of the clay. They made pots and jars to keep water in and to cook in. Bird-Ready-to-Fly often went with her mother, To-Dip-Water, to get clay for pots. They also brought back plants with which to make the colors and brushes used to decorate the pots.

The desert provided many plants used for all kinds of things. Mesquite wood made a fine, slow-burning fuel for cooking, or for a warm fire on cold nights. The Hopi used certain plants to make paints and dyes for coloring pots, baskets, or clothes. Some plants were cooked and eaten. Others were used to flavor foods. Bird-Ready-to-Fly had been taught what all these plants looked like, and she knew where to find them.

Indeed, everything the Peaceful Ones needed could be found in the desert. Of course, the one thing there was not much of in the desert was water. The Peaceful Ones built their villages near springs to have water for drinking and cooking. They planted their crops below the mesas, where water drained into the land.

The Peaceful Ones were farmers. Most of their food came from the land. Each clan, or group of related people, had its own land. The land belonged to the women of the clan, but the men did the farming.

Bird-Ready-to-Fly's father, Warming-by-the-Fire, spent much of his time in the fields. There was always a lot to do. In spring, he broke up the ground and planted the seed corn. He built little fences of stones and dried twigs and leaves. When the new plants began to peep up, the fences kept the wind from covering the plants with sand. Even so, some sand always blew through the fences. Then, he cleaned off the little plants very gently, and, of course, he pulled up weeds to give the little plants room to grow.

To grow tall and ripe, the corn and other crops needed rain. Rain was one of the most important things in the lives of the Peaceful Ones. Each year they held very special ceremonies to remind the spirits that rain was needed. Bird-Ready-to-Fly knew that it was the kachinas (kah CHEE nuhz)

who looked after the weather. The kachinas were
great spirits who lived in mountains to the west
and came to the Peaceful Ones during planting
season.

Sometimes, certain men dressed up as kachinas.
In one ceremony, they went from house to house,
asking if the children had been good for the past
year. They threatened to take the bad children
away in the baskets they carried with them.

Bird-Ready-to-Fly remembered last year's
Snake Dance very well. The priests of the Snake
and Antelope societies did this dance every other
year. They painted their bodies and wore special
costumes. As the whole village watched, the
priests danced and chanted.

The most important part came when the
snake priests performed a special dance with live

snakes held in their mouths or wrapped around their necks. At the end of this dance, the priests dropped the snakes onto a special design made of corn meal. Then they picked up the snakes and turned them loose outside the village. Everyone knew the snakes would hurry off to tell the spirits of the need for rain.

When Warming-by-the-Fire was not working on the farmland, he was always busy with other things. He might make a pair of moccasins or weave a blanket. The weaving of cloth, from cotton grown on the farms, was done only by men.

Sitting in the house in the evening, Warming-by-the-Fire might work at making a kachina doll or a prayer stick. The doll would be used for religious ceremonies, and Bird-Ready-to-Fly knew the kachina dolls were not toys to play with.

To make a prayer stick, Warming-by-the-Fire used a slim twig of cottonwood. He painted the stick and decorated it with feathers held in place by cotton cord. After breathing prayers onto the stick, he might place it at the village spring, or on the farmland, or up among the rafters of the house. The feathers would carry his prayers to the gods.

At times, Warming-by-the-Fire went to a large underground room called a kiva (KEE vuh). There were several kivas in the village. Only men could go to a kiva. Bird-Ready-to-Fly knew the men went there to talk. She also knew that the kiva was a place for special religious ceremonies.

Bird-Ready-to-Fly's mother, To-Dip-Water, was always busy, too. Now she was grinding dried corn into meal. Seeing Bird-Ready-to-Fly looking

at her, she smiled. "Come, help me grind the corn," she said.

Bird-Ready-to-Fly put her half-finished basket aside and joined her mother. First, To-Dip-Water spread kernels of corn on a rough, flat surface. She used a flat stone to rub and press the kernels into a coarse powder. Then Bird-Ready-to-Fly ground the coarse powder on two or more other stones, each time grinding until the corn meal was fine and smooth. As they worked, mother and daughter sang a corn-grinding song together.

Hopi Ways

The Hopi people ate corn as their main food. Hopi men grew the corn on little patches of farmland. Some of the corn was yellow, like most of the corn grown today, but the Hopi also grew red, purple, and even blue corn.

Hopi women roasted the kernels to dry them out, then ground them into powder, or corn meal. The women baked the corn meal into crispy wafers called *piki.* They also mixed it with water and cooked it in a pot. This made a mushy pudding without much taste.

Hopi men also grew beans and squash. The women collected many kinds of plants that grew wild in the desert. Some of these were eaten and some were used to add spicy flavors to food. The Hopi often put salt in their food. They got the salt from nearby mineral springs. Sometimes they sweetened their mushy corn meal pudding with the fruits of desert cactus plants.

The Hopi kept flocks of tame turkeys and ate turkey meat once in a while. They did not eat much other meat. There just were not enough animals in the desert to make it worth going hunting every day.

Hopi men often spent much of their time in an underground room called a kiva. It was a sort of special circular room for them. It was also used for religious ceremonies and special meetings. Women could not go into a kiva except on special occasions.

However, once in a while, all the men of a village would go on a hunt together. If they were lucky, they might bring back some deer, antelope, or rabbits. Then the Hopi women would make a meat stew to go with the usual piki and vegetables. This was a wonderful treat.

When a Hopi man got married, he went to live in his wife's house. Women owned all the houses in a Hopi village. They also did most of the work of building a house. Men only helped in the heavy part of the work. They carried rocks from the desert and put up the poles that held up the roof.

A Hopi house was just a single room. The walls were made of rocks piled on top of each other. The rocks were joined together and covered with plaster made of clay and water. Wooden poles were laid across the tops of the walls. Brush and dry grass were crammed between the poles and smeared with plaster to make the roof. The floor was also a thick coating of plaster.

The Hopi of today still live in such houses, in villages called pueblos. *Pueblo* (PWEHB loh) is a Spanish word meaning "village."

Hopi men carved and painted dolls that represented magical beings called kachinas.

Hopi women built the houses in which their families lived. They joined and covered the stones with a plaster made of clay and water.

Young Hopi girls wore a hairdo that looked like the flower of the squash plant. Married women wore their hair in two braids.

During the hot desert summers, a Hopi man wore only a sort of short skirt made of cotton. A woman wore a dress that was simply a square piece of cotton cloth. She wrapped the square around herself and fastened it over her right shoulder. Around her waist she wore a cloth belt. The Hopi men grew the cotton on the farms and wove it into cloth.

In colder weather, the Hopi wore moccasins of animal skin. The moccasins reached up to their ankles. Men would wrap themselves in cotton blankets. Both men and women wore robes made of rabbit fur.

Hopi men wove cotton into cloth for blankets and clothes.

How People Came into the World

A Hopi Legend

When the world was new, there was darkness everywhere. There were no people or animals. At that time, there were really four worlds. There was the world we know now and three cave worlds beneath it, one under the other. Above these four worlds lived the Spirit Masters.

The first people and animals came into the lowest cave world. They quickly filled the cave to overflowing. They bumped and pushed each other in the darkness. There was hardly enough room to turn around! The cave was soon filled with dirt and disorder. The people began to complain in loud voices.

The Spirit Masters said, "This is not good. Someone must see what can be done to make things better." Two of the Spirit Masters, who were brothers, said, "We will make it better."

The two brothers made a hole through the earth and through the roof of each cave. They then went down into the darkness of the lowest cave world. There, the brothers planted all the plants we have today. They hoped that one of the plants would grow tall and strong. The people and other

animals could then use it as a ladder to climb up into the second cave world.

Most of the plants did not grow very tall. Others were not strong enough, or could not be climbed, but one plant did grow through the hole in the roof of the cave. This plant made a fine ladder. It was jointed and easy to climb. It was the cane plant, a reed that grows near water. Ever since, the cane plant has grown in clusters along the Colorado River.

Many of the people and animals climbed up the cane plant into the second cave. This world was dark, too. The people could not tell how big the cave was. They feared it might be too small to hold all those who had been in the first cave. So they shook the ladder, knocking off those who were climbing up after them. Then they pulled the ladder up so that no one else could come up into the second cave world.

It was not long before the second cave was overcrowded, too. Then, some of the people and animals raised the cane ladder to the hole in the roof. They climbed up the ladder into the third cave world. Again, they pulled the ladder up so no one could follow.

The third cave was larger than the other two, but it was just as dark. So the two brothers found fire and showed the people how to make torches. In the light of the torches, the men set about building kivas.

While the people lived in the third cave world, an evil came upon them. A strange sickness struck the women. They began to dance, hour after hour, stopping only to sleep. They did not cook meals for their families or take care of their children. They only danced and slept.

The men decided that the people and animals must leave the third cave world. Again the cane ladder was raised to the hole in the roof. The people and the animals climbed up the ladder and through the hole, which is now called the Grand Canyon. They found themselves in the fourth world—the world in which we live.

This world, too, was dark, for at that time the sky covered the world like the roof of a cave. The world seemed damp and muddy. Even when the people lit torches, it was still too dark to see well.

The people, together with Spider, Coyote, Vulture, Swallow, and Locust, met to see how they might bring more light into the world. They decided that Spider should try first. So she spun a ball of pure white silk. It gave a little light, but not enough. The people put Spider's silk ball into the west, where it became the moon.

Then the people bleached a deerskin until it was pure white. They made it into a round shield that shone with brilliant light. They put the shield into the east. It became the sun. Now there was light in the world.

It so happened that while Coyote was in the cave world he had found a jar. He had brought this jar up into the fourth world with him, but the jar was heavy and he was tired of carrying it. He decided to leave it, but first he was curious to see what was in it.

Now that there was enough light to see by, he opened the jar. At once, a great many shining sparks flew out. The sparks scorched Coyote's face. This is why the coyote has a black face today. The shining sparks flew up into the sky and became the stars.

With all this light, the people could now see

the world very well. Water surrounded the small bit of land.

The people and animals urged Vulture to spread his wings and fan the water to make it roll away. Then there would be more land. Vulture did so. As the water flowed away to the east and west, huge mountains appeared in the distance.

To help the people and animals, the two brothers cut deep grooves in the mountains to let the water flow through. As the water rushed through the grooves, it made them deeper and deeper. This is how the great valleys of the world were formed. The water has flowed away ever since. This is why there is more and more land and why the world becomes drier and drier.

*P*eople of Peace

"Why do we call ourselves 'Peaceful Ones'?" the young Hopi boy wanted to know. "Didn't we ever fight a war?"

The old man, who was a priest of the Pueblo, smiled. "We have always believed that war is stupid, but we did fight a sort of a war, once."

"Who did we fight?" the boy demanded.

The old man lit a stubby pipe. "We fought against the Spaniards. The Spanish explorer Francisco Coronado came here in the year 1540. He and his men wanted gold. They did not find any. So, they left, but Coronado claimed our land for Spain!

"After a while, a Spanish governor came with many soldiers and priests. He told us that we all belonged to the king of Spain. The Spaniards brought horses, sheep, and goats, as well as fruit trees and pepper plants. These things were useful to us, but the Spaniards also made harsh laws and treated us unfairly. If we did not obey the laws, we were punished severely.

"The Spaniards also told us we had to give up our religion and accept their religion. Our religion has always meant a great deal to us. At one time, it was the most important thing in our lives. For some of us, it still is.

"We did not want to give up our religion, and we hated the unfair laws. People of different Pueblos met in secret to plan an uprising against the Spanish.

"Our leader was named Popé (poh PAY). He was a medicine man of the Tewa people, from the

The Hopi are excellent potters. This bowl is being painted with a yucca brush by a potter from Polacca, Arizona.

Pueblo of San Juan, not far from Santa Fe, New Mexico. News of when to strike was sent by runners. The runners carried a piece of knotted string that told us the day. On August 10, 1680, the Pueblo people rose up and attacked the Spaniards. We killed more than 400 of them. The others fled south to what is now El Paso, Texas. Then we burned the churches and houses the Spanish had built.

"Twelve years later, a Spanish army came with many soldiers who had guns and cannons. They fought our neighbors to the east and killed thousands of them. Those who survived moved west to live among us

"To be safe, we pretended to accept Spanish ways, but secretly, we kept our own. We had as little as possible to do with the Spaniards who were moving in on us.

"Then, in 1810, Mexico began a war to be free of Spanish rule. At the time, we were part of

Mexico. It took 11 years for the Mexicans to win their war. Their government passed laws that freed us and the other Indians of the Southwest.

"In the 1840's, the United States fought a war against Mexico. The Mexicans gave our land to the United States, and in 1912 it became part of the state of Arizona. The United States agreed to let us keep the land and our way of life. For the most part, that promise has been kept.

"Before the Spanish came, there were several thousand Hopi. The Spanish brought disease that killed many of us. But we recovered, and today, we number almost 12,000.

"Many Hopi still practice our ancient religion and follow the old ways. Some Hopi women prepare stone-ground corn for special occasions. We still make pottery, baskets, silver jewelry, and kachina dolls. At festivals, Hopi men dress as kachinas and dance in the village square. The Hopi are trying to recover ancient kachina dolls and other sacred objects that have been dug up from Hopi lands. They also want to stop the mining and polluting of their sacred lands." The old priest smiled wistfully at the boy, who was wearing a T-shirt, jeans, and sneakers. "But a lot of Hopi are becoming just like other Americans."

Dan Namingha

Dan Namingha, a Hopi born on May 1, 1950, comes from a family of famous pottery makers.

• As a child, Namingha sketched on everything, even the outside wall of his house.

• After art school, Namingha entered the Marine Corps to take a break from painting and think about his artistic goals. He realized his passion was portraying Native American culture through abstract shapes and colors.

• Exhibitions of his paintings and sculptures have toured worldwide.

The Aztec

City Dwellers of Mexico

The Aztec people lived in a broad valley in Central Mexico. Around 500 years ago, about 200,000 to 3000,000 people lived in the Aztec capital of Tenochtitlan (tay nohch TEE tlahn). Tenochtitlan was built on an island in a lake. Today, Mexico City stands there.

The emperor, the supreme ruler of all the Aztec, was a noble who was chosen by the other nobles. Most of the Aztec people had regular daily jobs. Many were farmers. Others were merchants, housebuilders, or metalworkers. There were also soldiers, priests, and government officials.

The Aztec had an advanced civilization. They had a number system and a kind of picture writing. They built huge temples and palaces. They borrowed many of their ideas from the Toltec, who lived in Mexico 300 years before them, as well as from the Maya of Central America.

The Aztec worshiped hundreds of gods and goddesses. War was considered a religious duty. They fought not only to enlarge their empire, but also to take prisoners to sacrifice to the gods. The Aztec armies conquered many of the people who lived near them.

North America

AZTEC

A Schoolboy of Tenochtitlan

It was the middle of the afternoon, the hottest part of the day. Spicy smells of cooking came from the houses of the city. The women were preparing the main meal of the day. From the House of the Young, the school that stood near the neighborhood temple, a crowd of boys burst forth. Their lessons over for a while, they were going home to eat.

One of the boys, Bee-in-the-Reeds, felt very proud of himself. His teacher, Fire Coyote, had praised him because he had remembered all the words of the sacred song the boys had learned that day. Not one of the other boys had done as well! In fact, one boy, who was a neighbor of Bee-in-the-Reeds, did so poorly he had been punished. He had been forced to breathe in smoke from burning chilis.

As Bee-in-the-Reeds walked along slowly, he could see the large, dark, cone shape of Popocatépetl, Smoking Mountain, in the distance. Its top was white with snow. Today, Smoking Mountain was quiet, but sometimes it rumbled loudly and poured out big, black clouds.

The narrow street ran alongside one of the city's many canals. As usual, the canal was filled with canoes. As Bee-in-the-Reeds stopped to look at them, someone pushed quickly past him. He turned and saw it was the boy who had been punished at school. "Ha, ha, soot face!" Bee-in-the-Reeds yelled.

The boy hung his head in shame and hurried on. He would probably be punished again when he got home.

Bee-in-the-Reeds soon reached his house. Like the other houses nearby, it sat at the edge of seven or eight long, narrow islands that stretched out into the water. The people had made these islands by piling mud inside of shallow, oblong barriers made of woven plant materials. Rows of trees planted at the edges of the islands kept the barriers in place. All of the mud in the islands came from the bottom of the lake.

Bee-in-the-Reed's father, Angry Turkey, was a farmer. On these long strips of moist, rich soil he grew corn, tomatoes, and other plants. The mud from the lake was so rich he could raise several different crops a year.

The family was ready to eat when Bee-in-the-Reeds came into the house. Everyone sat on woven mats on the floor, around the cooking fire. His little sister, Jade Doll, grinned at him as she munched on a tlaxcalli. His mother, Blue Corn Flower, handed him a tlaxcalli, too. He rolled it into a tube and scooped up a mouthful of beans with it.

"My teacher complimented me today," Bee-in-the-Reeds proudly told his parents. "I was the only one who knew all the words of the song to the Corn Goddess!"

"That is good," said his father. "It is important to know the songs that honor the gods. Are you also learning to use your weapons well?"

"I am getting better," answered Bee-in-the-Reeds, his mouth full of food. "Fire Coyote says so."

"Work hard at it," his father told him. "When you grow up and become a warrior, I want you to take an enemy prisoner. That is what I did when I was a warrior. We need many prisoners so that we can sacrifice them to the gods."

Bee-in-the-Reeds finished his tlaxcalli. Because he was 12 years old, he was allowed to have half of another tlaxcalli. He scooped up as many beans as he could with it, and crammed it into his mouth.

"Do not put it all into your mouth at once!" his mother scolded.

Bee-in-the-Reeds took a long drink of water. The meal was now over. If his family had been wealthy, or nobles, they would all take a long nap, but common people had no time for such luxury. They had too much work to do.

Bee-in-the-Reeds spent the rest of the day helping his father and learning from him. Jade Doll, who was only 4, helped her mother around the house, learning from her. By the time Jade Doll was 16, she would know how to cook, make thread, weave cloth, and care for a house. She would be ready to marry a young man picked by her parents.

At the age of 15, Bee-in-the-Reeds would spend most of his time at a military school. He would even sleep there at night. He would be taught to be a soldier and would fight in battles. In time, his parents would pick a girl for him to marry. Then, he would probably become a farmer, like his father.

But, if he were a very good soldier and took many prisoners, Bee-in-the-Reeds could become a commander. That might make him wealthy. He dreamed of becoming an Eagle Knight, in a feathered costume and eagle helmet. He could wear a colorful cloak, a gold ornament in his nose, and a carved jade plug in his lower lip. Then everyone would know how brave he was!

But that was years ahead. Right now, he had to help his father plant chili peppers.

Aztec Ways

The way an Aztec dressed depended upon who he was and what he did. Aztec clothes showed if someone was a worker, a high official, a brave soldier, or a rich merchant in Aztec society.

A farmer or worker wore a breechclout and a short cloak of rough white cloth made from plant leaves. His wife wore a plain white skirt that reached to her ankles, and a pullover shirt. Children dressed like their parents—boys in breechclouts and cloaks, and girls in skirts and shirts. Working men, women, and children went barefoot.

A wealthy Aztec, such as a merchant, dressed a bit differently. A man still wore a breechclout, but it was made of cotton, and it was often decorated with designs. He also wore a cloak of white cotton, tied over his shoulder. Wealthy people usually wore sandals made of woven plant leaves or leather.

Noblemen and very rich men wore cloaks that were dyed bright colors and decorated with designs. A rich man with many cloaks might wear several at a time, one on top of another. This showed how wealthy he was.

The way a soldier dressed showed how brave he was. Soldiers who were especially brave could become Jaguar Knights or Eagle Knights. A Jaguar Knight wore the skin of a jaguar, with the jaguar's head over his own. An Eagle Knight wore a feathered costume and a helmet shaped like the head of an eagle with an open beak.

A common soldier usually wore sandals, a breechclout, and a padded short-sleeved shirt that reached to his knees. If he had never captured a prisoner in battle, he kept his head shaved, except for a clump of hair at the back. A man who had captured an enemy could wear long hair and a decorated cloak. A man who had taken several prisoners could also wear special ear and lip ornaments and other decorations.

The Aztec wore many kinds of jewelry. Rich people wore golden necklaces, armbands, ear decorations, and gold or jade rods through their nose or lower lip. Poor people wore ornaments of stone or sea shell.

The emperor was the most beautifully dressed of all. He had

There was rejoicing when Aztec soldiers brought in prisoners after a battle. The prisoners would be sacrificed to the Aztec gods. Strange as it may seem, the prisoners were proud and willing to be sacrificed. They believed that they would then go to feed the gods and make them strong.

cloaks made of colored feathers, of coyote fur, and of many different colors of cloth. His cloth cloaks were trimmed with feathers and decorated with designs. Only the emperor could wear a nose ornament made of the greenish-blue stone we call turquoise. Also, only the emperor was allowed to wear a turquoise-colored cloak.

The house of an Aztec worker or farmer was a small hut, shaped like a rectangle. It had a low

Every Aztec city and town had a marketplace. There, shoppers bought food, clothes, and other things. For money, the Aztec used a variety of items, including gold dust, pieces of copper, and cacao beans.

doorway, but no windows. The floor was just the ground. Some houses were made of dried clay bricks. Others were made of poles and plant stems woven together and smeared with wet clay. The clay dried into a hard plaster. Most houses had slanted roofs made of dried plants.

On the floor would be a few woven mats for sitting and for sleeping. One or two wooden chests held clothes and other belongings. Baskets, cooking pots, and other things used every day were piled against the walls. There would be several statues of gods, made of wood, stone, or clay.

In the middle of the floor was the "stove." It was a round, flat plate made of dried clay. It sat on three large stones. A fire was built under it. It was used for cooking tlaxcallis and other kinds of food.

The house of a wealthy Aztec was often a small palace. It might have a dining room, a kitchen, separate rooms for each member of the family, rooms for servants, storerooms, and a large room for entertaining. The walls were made of stone or clay, covered with plaster. Walls were often painted in colorful designs. The doorway of each room was often covered with a cloth curtain.

The floor of such a house was made of a sort of cement. The roof, made of rows of logs covered with plaster, was flat. Many wealthy

Aztec covered their roofs with earth and planted gardens on them.

Several special rooms in the house had no roof. These rooms were like little inside yards, where people spent much of their time.

The Aztec emperor and many wealthy nobles had two-story houses. These houses had large rooms and yards, but even rich people did not have much more furniture.

Have you ever eaten a tlaxcalli (tlaks KAH lee)? If you have, you probably didn't know it. Tlaxcalli is the Nahuatl (Aztec) word for tortilla (tawr TEE yuh), a thin, flat, pancake made of corn meal mixed with water. Another Aztec food you may have eaten is the tamale (tuh MAH lee). A tamale is a thick, mushy, corn-meal pancake. It is spread with a thick coat of cooked meat or vegetables, then rolled up. Women dried ears of corn and ground the kernels into coarse powder, or corn meal, for tamales, tlaxcallis, and other corn-based foods.

Aztec workers ate breakfast at around mid-morning. This was usually just a bowl of cornmeal mixed with water—a mushy pudding. The main meal was eaten in the middle of the afternoon. At this meal, people usually had something such as tlaxcallis and beans in a spicy sauce.

People used the tlaxcallis as spoons. They rolled them up and dipped them into the beans. A 4- or 5-year-old could have one tlaxcalli at a meal. A 6- to 12-year-old could have 1½ tlaxcallis. A 13-year-old was allowed to eat two.

Most Aztec never ate much meat. They could not afford it. For a special occasion, however, they might buy a turkey or a small dog at the market.

The emperor and nobles had more and better food than workers. They ate such things as stewed ducks, fish in a sauce of tomatoes and chili peppers, and other tasty dishes. With their meals, they drank a frothy drink made of whipped chocolate flavored with honey or vanilla.

Aztec Gods

The Aztec believed that a god or goddess controlled the sun, rain, wind, flowers, fire, and so on. So, they had dozens of gods and goddesses to worship.

One of the most important gods to the Aztec was Quetzalcóatl (keht sahl koh AH tl), god of life and learning, who had created the human race. Another important god was Huitzilopochtli (wee tsee loh POHCH tlee), god of the sun and of war.

The Aztec thought that these two gods, and many others, looked like humans. Other gods and goddesses, such as Coatlique (koh aht LEE kway), the earth goddess, were horrible monsters.

Coatlique

Quetzalcóatl

Huitzilopochtli

The End of an Empire

"My brother is a student at the University of Mexico," Consuela told her friend, Ramon. "He is studying about the Aztec. Some of our ancestors were Aztec."

"All of my ancestors were Spanish—I think," Ramon declared.

Consuela giggled. "Lots of mine were, too. It's funny, because at first, the Spaniards and Aztec fought each other!

"My brother says the first Spanish explorers came to Mexico in 1517. They found gold ornaments in some of the villages. Soon, other explorers came, looking for gold. In 1519, Hernando Cortés landed in Mexico with 600 men. Cortés heard of the great Aztec city of Tenochtitlan. He was sure he would find gold there.

"When the Spaniards got to Tenochtitlan, the Aztec emperor, Montezuma II, greeted them with gifts. The Spaniards, afraid because the Aztec outnumbered them, seized Montezuma and made him their prisoner.

"The Spaniards ruled the city for about six months. Then, while Cortés was away, the Aztec revolted. The Spaniards had to fight their way to safety. Montezuma was killed. So were many Spaniards.

"Spanish reinforcements arrived, and thousands of people the Aztec had conquered joined Cortés. With this big army, Cortés attacked Tenochtitlan.

"For several months there was terrible fighting. Thousands of Aztec were killed. Finally, they had to give up. The Spaniards destroyed Tenochtitlan and started building

Mexico City was built atop the ruins of the great Aztec city of Tenochtitlan. The Aztec sculptures shown in this photo were excavated from the construction site of this Mexico City subway as it was being built.

what is now Mexico City atop the ruins. The Aztec had to obey Spanish laws and live as ordered by the Spaniards. Many Aztec were forced to work for the Spaniards, almost as slaves. After a time, however, Spaniards and Aztecs married one another. They became one people—Mexicans.

"The Aztec empire was gone but not forgotten. Scientists who study ancient ruins went digging in Mexico City and uncovered the Aztec's Great Temple. On the outskirts of the city, they discovered more temples and a palace.

"Temples and palaces are only the grandest remnants of Aztec culture. Words are another. Náhuatl (NAH wah tl), the Aztec language, is still spoken by many of the people in small villages near Mexico City. However, you do not have to visit Mexico to hear bits of the Aztec language. The words tomato, chocolate, and avocado all come from the Aztec language as do many place names, such as Acapulco and Mexico."

Native North Americans Today

The ways of life of the Native North Americans of hundreds of years ago are changed forever. Today's Native North Americans live in a world that is very different from the one their ancestors knew.

To many Native North Americans, the old ways still seem best. They try to live as their ancestors lived. As much as possible, they try to keep apart from the modern world around them.

For other Native North Americans, today's world seems best. They are proud to be Native North Americans, but they want to live in the same way most other people live. They do not want to be thought of as "different."

Still other Native North Americans—many of them—try to mix the old ways and new ways. They want to keep many of their old customs and ways of life, but they also want to take advantage of the science and technology of the modern world.

As you will see, Native North Americans today live in many different ways in many different places. You will see what they do and how many are trying to preserve their culture. You will also see how young Native North Americans live and how many are interested in learning about their heritage and passing it on to future generations.

Today, about 2,400,000 Indians live in the United States. Almost half of them live on reservations. The nation's approximately 285 federal and state Indian reservations cover over 58 million acres (20 million hectares) in about 30 states. Canada has more than 2,200 areas, called *reserves,* set aside for Indians. Often, these are places where their people have lived for hundreds of years, and where many Native North American tribes have their own governments. Many Indians who live on reservations follow their tribe's traditional way of life.

Most other Indians living in the United States make their homes in towns and cities. These members of the Onondaga Nation, *top,* work to clean up their community during their annual spring clean-up in Syracuse, New York.

A Quinault father and daughter, *bottom left, opposite,* unload their fishing catch from a boat on the Quinault Indian Reservation in Taholah, Washington. The Northwest Coast Indians have long enjoyed a plentiful supply of fish from nearby waters.

A storm gathers over Laguna Pueblo, New Mexico, *left.* Laguna Pueblo has six villages and is one of the largest Keresan pueblos.

Two Navajo boys, *below,* play basketball at Monument Valley Navajo Tribal Park on the Utah/Arizona border. The park is entirely within the Navajo Indian Reservation. About 150,000 people live on the reservation, the nation's largest (16 million acres [6.5 million hectares]).

Native North Americans do all kinds of work. Many are farmers, sheep or cattle herders, fishermen, or lumberjacks. Others are doctors, lawyers, politicians, scientists, professors, factory workers, artists, and entertainers.

This Mescalero Apache firefighter, *above,* watches a controlled burn on Mescalero Apache Indian Reservation in New Mexico. The cooler evening temperatures reduce the risk of fire racing out of control and burning homes on the reservation. Today, many Apache work for tribal-owned industries and lumber or cattle companies.

A Navajo Agricultural Products Industry official, *right,* inspects a plant on a reservation near Farmington, New Mexico. Large numbers of Navajo are farmers or sheep ranchers, but others are engineers, miners, teachers, or technicians.

A district court judge of the Muskogee (Creek) Nation, *right,* serves his community in Okmulgee, Oklahoma. Tribal councils help govern the various tribes and supervise their property. Today, many Creeks are poor. But others work in a wide range of fields, including education, law, and medicine.

A Pueblo blackjack dealer, *left,* deals cards at a casino on the Sandia Pueblo in northern New Mexico. Casinos provide many tribes with an important source of income and aid other businesses such as craftwork and tourism.

A Seminole air boat operator, *right,* leads a Seminole swamp tour on Big Cypress Reservation in Florida. Florida Seminole make a living by hunting, fishing, farming, raising cattle, or working in tourism or other industries.

For most Native North Americans, the past is precious. Many are trying to keep the language, dances, music, and arts of their ancestors.

A Zuni artist, *above,* paints a mural on the wall of Our Lady of Guadalupe Church, Zuni Pueblo, New Mexico. The series of murals features paintings of traditional Zuni kachina ceremonial figures, tribal leaders, and traditional crops, birds, and animals.

Navajo are skilled at weaving wool blankets. This woman, *below,* weaves a blanket at her home on a Navajo reservation near Farmington, New Mexico. Indian craftwork is a source of income and a way of preserving Native American culture.

Northwest Coast Indian groups, *top right, opposite,* participate in the opening ceremonies of the North American Indigenous Games at Inner Harbour in Victoria, British Columbia, Canada. Held every three years, the games feature native peoples from

North America competing in such traditional Indian sports and activities as running, lacrosse, kayaking, canoeing, and archery.

Many young Native North Americans look to their parents, grandparents, and other adults

from their native group to help teach them to carry on their native culture and traditions. A Pueblo woman, *above,* in Cahiti Pueblo, New Mexico, teaches her granddaughter to bake bread in a *horno,* a traditional outdoor oven.

A Cherokee father and daughter, *right,* chip knife blades at the Cherokee Heritage Center in Talequah, Oklahoma. Cherokee culture has remained strong and today the Cherokee are the largest Indian tribe in the United States.

Many young Native North Americans today are just like other young people across North America. But many are doing things in much the same ways their ancestors did. And many are interested in learning about and preserving their culture.

This Native American boy, *left*, dances in a competition during a powwow at Mille Lacs Reservation in Minnesota. Modern powwows are more festive versions of the traditional tribal meetings held to discuss problems. These gatherings bring tribes together to celebrate their heritage and feature dancing, singing, arts, and crafts.

Playing a game much like one their ancestors played hundreds of years ago, these Onondaga Iroquois boys, *left*, compete in lacrosse on a reservation in Nedrow, New York.

Two Inuit girls, *above,* study the Inuit language on a computer at a school in Igloolik, Nunavut, Canada. Today, fewer than 200 Native American languages are spoken. Only about 40 of the languages are spoken by people of all ages, including children.

Woodcarving has long been a specialty of the Northwest Coast Indians. A Tsimshian man, *left,* teaches his son the traditional art of totem pole carving in Kingston, Washington. The family and clan symbols carved into the pole help preserve the clan's history for new generations.

Native North Americans Today   197

Indian IQ

Join one or more friends in raising your Indian IQ (Information Quotient). As you go around the board, you will review some facts you have read and learn new facts, too.

To play:

1 With a marker, draw two rings around one toothpick and a single ring around two other toothpicks.

2 Hide the three marked toothpicks in one or both of your hands by making two fists. Have another player choose a hand.

3 If the hand the player chooses is empty, he or she skips a turn. Otherwise, he or she counts the rings on the toothpicks in the selected hand, and moves his or her button forward that many spaces on the board.

4 The player follows the instructions in the space on which he or she lands.

5 Take turns repeating steps 1 through 4 until each player reaches FINISH. The player with the most toothpicks at the finish is the winner.

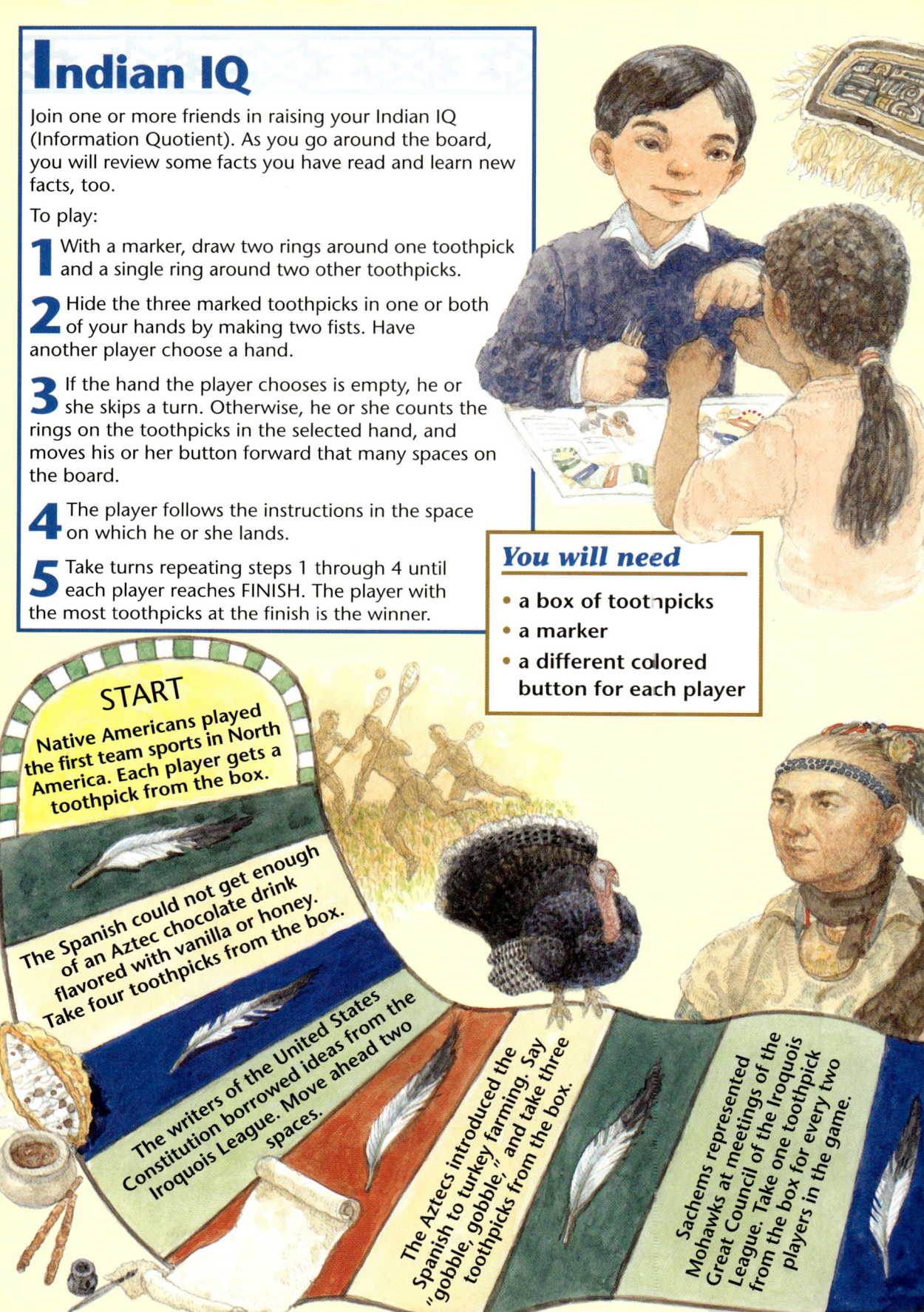

START
Native Americans played the first team sports in North America. Each player gets a toothpick from the box.

The Spanish could not get enough of an Aztec chocolate drink flavored with vanilla or honey. Take four toothpicks from the box.

The writers of the United States Constitution borrowed ideas from the Iroquois League. Move ahead two spaces.

The Aztecs introduced the Spanish to turkey farming. Say "gobble, gobble," and take three toothpicks from the box.

Sachems represented Mohawks at meetings of the Great Council of the Iroquois League. Take one toothpick from the box for every two players in the game.

FINISH

The weave in some Pomo baskets is so tight that a magnifying glass must be used to count the stitches. Count the number of toothpicks all other players have and take that many from the box.

Tlingit trading partners paid high prices for the Chilkat blankets that Tlingit women wove from cedar-bark fiber and wool. Offer to pay toothpicks to trade spaces with another player.

A group of Alaskan Inuit developed the malamute—a strong, rugged sled dog. Fetch a toothpick from the box.

The Blackfeet used dried buffalo meat, fat, and chokecherries to make pemmican—an early kind of trail mix. Take two toothpicks.

French traders introduced metal axes and knives to the Osage. Trade all your toothpicks for another player's.

The Northeast Woodland Indians taught the French how to make snowshoes. If you can bend one of your toothpicks without breaking it, take two toothpicks from the box.

The Osage served as scouts for the United States Army in the 1860's. Find out what lies ahead. Move to the space in front of the lead player. If you are in the lead, stay put.

Sioux Charles Eastman helped start the Boy Scouts. Do a good deed. Give a toothpick to another player.

Indian Influence: the States and Provinces

States with Names of Native American Origin

State	Origin
1. Alabama	name of a Native American group called the Alibama, meaning "clearers of thickets"
2. Alaska	Aleut word for "great country"
3. Arizona	Pima word for "place of the little spring"
4. Arkansas	Algonquian word for "south wind"
5. Connecticut	Mohican word for "on the long river"
6. Illinois	Algonquian word meaning "great men"
7. Iowa	Iowa tribe, whose name means "here I rest" or "beautiful land"
8. Kansas	Sioux word for "south wind people"
9. Kentucky	Cherokee word meaning "meadowland" or "land of tomorrow"
10. Massachusetts	Massachusetts word meaning "great hill"
11. Michigan	Ojibwa words for "great water"
12. Minnesota	Dakota Sioux word for "sky-tinted water"
13. Mississippi	Ojibwa words for "gathering-in of all the waters"
14. Missouri	Algonquian words for "river of the big canoes"
15. Nebraska	Oto word meaning "shallow water"
16. (North and South) Dakota	Sioux word for "friend" or "ally"
17. Ohio	Iroquois word for "good river"
18. Oklahoma	Choctaw word for "red people"
19. Oregon	Shoshone word meaning "place of identity"
20. Tennessee	from the name of a Cherokee village
21. Texas	Caddo word for "friends" or "allies"
22. Utah	Navajo word for "higher up"
23. Wisconsin	Ojibwa word for "grassy place"
24. Wyoming	Delaware word for "on the great plains"

States and Provinces with Largest Native American Populations

1. California	6. British Columbia
2. Oklahoma	7. Manitoba
3. Arizona	8. Texas
4. New Mexico	9. Saskatchewan
5. Ontario	10. North Carolina

Largest Groups of Native North Americans Today

1. Cherokee	6. Inuit
2. Navajo	7. Pueblo
3. Sioux	8. Apache
4. Ojibwa	9. Lumbee
5. Choctaw	10. Iroquois

Canadian Provinces and Territories with Names of Native American Origin

Province/Territory	Origin
1. Manitoba	Cree word meaning "the strait of the great spirit"
2. Nunavut	Inuit word meaning "our land"
3. Quebec	Algonquin word for "where the river narrows"
4. Saskatchewan	Cree word meaning "fast-flowing river"
5. Yukon	Athbascan word meaning "great river"

Glossary

Anasazi (AH nuh SAH zee) The ancestors of modern-day Pueblo Indians. Sometimes called the *cliff dwellers* or *Ancestral Puebloans.*

angekok (ANG guh kok) An Inuit who has special powers to heal.

Anishinabe (ah nihsh ih NAH bay) One of the largest tribal groups in North America that once lived along the shores of Lake Superior and Lake Huron. The word means "First People."

anorak (AH nuh rahk) An Inuit jacket made of sealskin, caribou hide, or animal fur, worn with the fur facing out.

bola (BOH luh) A rope with weights at both ends. Bolas were used by the Inuit to catch game.

camass (KAM uhs) A wild plant of the lily family that grows in western North America. Some Indians eat its sweet, nourishing bulbs. It is sometimes called wild hyacinth.

caribou (KAR uh boo) A large North American deer hunted by the Inuit in the spring and fall.

flint (flihnt) A very hard, gray or brown, granular quartz that makes a spark when struck against steel. Indians used flint for arrowheads and to start fires.

Inuit (IHN yoo iht) A people who live in the Arctic regions of North America and northeastern Asia. The singular of Inuit is *Inuk.*

harpoon (hahr POON) An arrow-shaped weapon with a rope tied to it. It is used for catching whales and other sea animals. It is either thrown by hand or fired from a gun.

kachina (kah CHEE nuh) The name of a religious ceremony of the Hopi and of carved wooden dolls used in the ceremony. The dolls represent spirits.

kayak (KY ak) An Inuit canoe made of animal skins stretched over a light frame of wood or bone, with an opening in the middle for a person.

kiva (KEE vuh) A ceremonial underground room of the Hopi.

moccasin (MOK uh suhn) A soft shoe often made from the skin of a deer and originally worn by North American Indians.

Náhuatl (NAH wah tuhl) The Aztec language.

narwhal (NAHR hwuhl) A type of whale of the Arctic seas. It has only two teeth.

pemmican (PEHM uh kuhn) A hard, chewy food of many Native North Americans that is made from dried meat pounded together with fat and berries or chokecherries.

persimmon (puhr SIHM uhn) The fruit of a North American tree that is very bitter when green, but sweet and good to eat when very ripe.

potlatch (PAHT lach) A great feast given by a wealthy Tlingit man in which he would give away much of his wealth.

Quetzalcóatl (keht SAHL koh AH tul) An Aztec god of life and learning. Aztecs believe Quetzalcóatl created the human race.

tamale (tuh MAH lee) A thick, mushy corn-meal pancake.

Tenochtitlan (tay nohch TEE tlahn) Capital of the Aztec empire, which stood at the site of present-day Mexico City.

tlaxcalli (tlaks KAH lee) A thin, flat pancake made of corn meal mixed with water. Today it is known by the Spanish name, tortilla.

umiak (OO mee ak) A large, open Inuit boat made of skins covering a wooden or bone frame and worked by paddles.

Find Out More

The Algonquin of New York
by David Oestreicher (Rosen Publishing Group, 2003)

This well-illustrated volume describes the origins, history, and culture of the Algonquins who lived in the area now known as New York state. The book includes a timeline following this Native American group from prehistory to the present. Other groups covered in this "Library of Native Americans" series include the Caddo, Chumash, Essselen, Iroquois, Kiowa, Luiseno, Ohlone, Oneida, Pomo, Potawatomi, and the Tongva.

Anasazi Culture at Mesa Verde
by Sabrina Crewe and Dale Anderson (Gareth Stevens, 2003)

This book is a great introduction to the Anasazi culture and its Mesa Verde cliff dwellings. It attempts to answer in simple language some of the many questions that are asked about this unique agricultural people who mysteriously disappeared.

Apache
edited by Marla Felkins Ryan and Linda Scmittroth (Blackbirch Press, 2002)

An introduction to the Apache people, this book covers the origins, history, culture, and customs of this southwestern group. Color illustrations, as well as maps and graphs, are included in this and the other volumes in this "Tribes of Native America" series. Other tribes covered are Blackfeet, Cahuilla, Cherokee, Cheyenne, Choctaw, Comanche, Cree, Crow, Hopi, Lakota, Mohawk, Narragansett, Navajo, Nez Perce, Ojibwa, Pomo, Seminole, Shawnee, Shoshone, Ute, and Zuni Pueblo.

Daily Life in a Plains Indian Village, 1868
by Michael Bad Hand Terry (Clarion Books, 1999)

Readers will get a good idea of what the Plains Indians of this time period wore, what everyday objects they used, what their daily life was like, and how their social organization worked. The historical background of this group is also included in this introduction to Plains Indian life.

Eyewitness: Aztec, Inca & Maya
by Elizabeth Baquedano (DK Publishing, 2000)

This "Eyewitness" series book chronicles the history, beliefs, and everyday lives of the ancient Aztec, Inca, and Maya peoples. Heavily illustrated.

Eyewitness: North American Indian
by David Murdock (DK Publishing, 2000)

This richly illustrated book from the "Eyewitness" series is an overview of the North American Indian. It covers the various groups and provides information on their customs, clothing, weapons, and tools.

The First Americans
http://www.germantown.k12.il.us/html/intro.html

This Web site is set up especially for students. It provides information about the homes, food, and clothing of the first Americans, as well as other interesting facts about their different cultures. There are also links to general information about Native Americans, as well as links to Indian legends.

Following the Great Herds: the Plains Indians and the American Buffalo
by Ryan P. Randolph (PowerKids Press, 2003)

In this short book, readers will learn about the Plains Indians and how they killed only as many buffalo as they needed. With westward expansion and the arrival of white settlers, mass killing of these animals took place. Tensions between the two groups rose and led to war.

The Inuit of Canada
by Danielle Corriveau (Lerner, 2002)

Maps and color photos fill this volume from the "First Peoples" series. This and the other books in the series (Cherokee, Choctaw, Iroquois, Navajo, Ojibwa, Pueblo, Seminole, Shoshone, and Sioux) explain to the reader how plants, animals, and the climate of the region had an impact on the daily life of the native tribes. The natives' adaptation to modern life is also discussed.

More than Moccasins:
A Kid's Activity Guide to Traditional North American Life
by Laurie M. Carlson (Chicago Review Press, 1994)

Children will learn about Native American life and values as they work through some of the 100 crafts and activities in this book. All are well illustrated and easy to follow.

Native-American Folk Tales
VHS 22 minutes (Shenandoah Film Productions)

With music and colorful animation, four Native American tales are told. "Storytelling Stone" comes from the Seneca tribe, "Pelican Girl" is from the Pacific Coastal Miwok group, "The Boy who Loved Bears" is a Pawnee tale, and "The Turkey Girl" is a southwestern tale from the Pueblo culture.

North American Indian Games
by Madelyn Anderson (Franklin Watts, 2000)

This book examines the origins, nature, and importance of games played by Native North Americans. Included are ball games, dice games, and guessing games.

Ojibwa: People of the Great Lakes
by Anne M. Todd (Bridgestone Books, 2003)

This book from the "American Indian Nations" series covers the life of the Ojibwa today as well as the history and traditions of the group. A timeline and a recipe are also included. Other groups covered in this series are Apache, Arapaho, Blackfeet, Cherokee, Cheyenne, Chumash, Comanche, Creek, Iroquois, Pawnee, Powhatan, Pueblo, Seminole, Sioux, and the Wampanoag.

The Potawatomi
by Karen Bush Gibson (Bridgestone Books, 2003)

This illustrated book geared for the young report writer includes simply stated information on the history, lifestyles, language, customs, religion, food, and clothing of the Potawatomi. This title includes instructions for a tribal throwing game called "Woodpecker." Other titles in this "Native Peoples" series include *The Apsaalooke (Crow) Nation, The Utes, The Cree Tribe,* and *The Osage.*

The Seminole
by Stefanie Takacs

This "True Book" is a simple introduction to the early history of the Seminole and its daily life in the 1800's. Readers will also learn about the Seminoles' culture and customs, their years of struggle, and about the Seminole of the 21st century. Check out other North American Indian titles in this series.

Tales from the Keeper of Myths:
Cherokee Stories for Children
by Shirley G. Webb (Universe, 2003, paper)

Storytelling was an important way for Native Americans to keep alive their traditions. The stories in this collection are based on authentic Cherokee legends and include tales of adventure and friendship.

The Tlingit
by Raymond Bial (Benchmark Books, 2003)

This title from the "Lifeways" series profiles the history, society, and culture of Alaska's Tlingit Indians. In addition, readers will find a timeline, a recipe, a language lesson, and two traditional stories. Other groups in this well-illustrated series include Apache, Blackfeet, Cherokee, Cheyenne, Choctaw, Comanche, Haida, Huron, Inuit, Iroquois, Mandan, Navajo, Nez Perce, Ojibwa, Powhatan, Pueblo, Seminole, Shoshone, and Sioux.

Totem Poles:
Art from the Pacific Northwest
http://members.aol.com/Art1234567/Totemart. html

On this Web site students will get information on these beautiful works of art that are made from giant trees. Includes crafts.

Index

This index is an alphabetical list of important topics covered in this book. It will help you find information given in both words and pictures. To help you understand what an entry means, there is sometimes a helping word in parentheses, for example, **angekoks** (healers). If there is information in both words and pictures, you will see the words *with pictures* in parentheses after the page number. If there is only a picture, you will see the word *picture* in parentheses after the page number.

Illustration Acknowledgments

The publishers of *Childcraft* gratefully acknowledge the courtesy of the following photographers, illustrators, agencies, and organizations for the photographs and illustrations in this volume. When all the illustrations for a sequence of pages are from a single source, the inclusive page numbers are given. Credits should be read from left to right, top to bottom, on their respective pages. All illustrations are the exclusive property of the publisher of *Childcraft* unless names are marked with an asterisk (*).

Covers:
 Aristocrat, Discovery, International and Standard Bindings: John Sandford
Heritage Binding: John Sandford; Jerry Pinkney; © Chuck West*; Krystyna Stasiak; © Kit Breen*; George Suyeoka; © Chicago Historical Society*; Richard Hook; © Independence National Historical Park*
Rainbow Binding: © Swift, Vanuga Images/Corbis*; John Sandford; George Suyeoka; Krystyna Stasiak
 1 Kinuko Craft
 2 Richard Hook
 5 Jerry Pinkney
 8–9 Richard Hook
 11 Tom Root, Serpent Mound State Memorial, Ohio Historical Society*
 12 National Park Service*
 14–24 John Sandford
 26 © First Light*
 27 © Bryan & Cherry Alexander*
 28–29 Ben Manchipp
 31–34 Kinuko Craft
 35–39 Michael Hampshire
 41–43 Krystyna Stasiak
 44–45 AP/Wide World*
 46–47 Ben Manchipp
 49–57 Richard Hook
 58–61 John Sandford
 63–65 Roberta Polfus
 66 Independence National Historical Park*
 67 © Roger La Borde*
 68–69 Ben Manchipp
 70–77 Richard Hook
 79 © Burstein Collection/Corbis*

 80–83 Dan B. Timmons
 85 *The Trail of Tears* (1942) oil on canvas by Robert Lindneux; The Woolaroc Museum*
 86 © Charlie Soap*
 88–89 Ben Manchipp
 91–99 Richard Hook
 100 John Sandford, Richard Hook
 102 *An Osage Indian Lancing a Buffalo* (1846–1848) oil on canvas by George Catlin; National Museum of American Art, Smithsonian Institution (Art Resource)*
 103 Chicago Historical Society*
 104–105 Ben Manchipp
 107–109 Jerry Pinkney
 110–115 Charles McBarron
 116 John Sandford, John S. Walter
 118 *Return of the Horse Thieves* (1900) watercolor by Charles M. Russell; C. M. Russell Museum*
 120 AP/Wide World*
 121 © Kit Breen*
 122–123 Ben Manchipp
 125–130 Kinuko Craft
 133 John Sandford
 134–135 John Dawson
 136 Jean Helmer
 137 © Nancy Simmerman*
 139 © Lawrence Migdale*
 140–141 Ben Manchipp
 142–144 Kinuko Craft
 146–149 John Dawson
 151 Krystyna Stasiak

 153 © Angel Wynn, Nativestock.com*
 154–155 Ben Manchipp
 157–160 Kinuko Craft
 162–165 John Dawson
 167–170 Krystyna Stasiak
 172 © Stephen Trimble*
 173 © Chuck West*
 174–175 Ben Manchipp
 177–183 Michael Hampshire
 185 George Suyeoka
 187 © Bob Frerck, Odyssey Productions*
 189 © Kit Breen*
 190–191 © Randi Anglin, The Image Works*; © Natalie Fobes, Corbis*; © Steve Warble, Mountain Magic Photography*; © Will Powers*
 192–193 © Raymond Gehman, Corbis*; © Randall Hyman*; © Ben Klaffke*; © Miguel Gandert, Corbis © Angel Wynn, Nativestock.com*
 194–195 © Michael R. Stoklos*; © Randall Hyman*; © Gunter Marx*; © Lawrence Migdale*; © Kit Breen*
 196–197 © Ralph LaPlant, North Wind Images*; © Lawrence Migdale*; © Bryan & Cherry Alexander*; © Lawrence Migdale*
 198–199 John Sandford